Praise for James Baldwin's

The Devil Finds Work

"His instructive comments reveal what a black child and black audiences in general perceive in white-produced movies, particularly those with biracial parts. . . . Typical Baldwin eloquence tinged with religious fervor."   —*Booklist*

"It is James Baldwin testifying honestly to his own experience at the movies. It is *his* experience and as such it either makes us see a point of view we are unlikely to have seen before (if we happen to be white) or confirms a way of looking at things for which we are unlikely to have gotten public affirmation (if we happen to be black)."   —Christopher Lehmann-Haupt, *The New York Times*

"Moralistic fervor, a high literary seriousness, the authority of the survivor, of the witness—these qualities made Baldwin unique."
                          —*The New York Review of Books*

"A provocative discussion."   —*Saturday Review*

JAMES BALDWIN

The Devil Finds Work

James Baldwin was born in 1924. He is the author of more than twenty works of fiction and nonfiction. Among the awards he received are a Eugene F. Saxon Memorial Trust Award, a Rosenwald Fellowship, a Guggenheim Fellowship, a *Partisan Review* Fellowship, and a Ford Foundation grant. He was made a Commander of the Legion of Honor in 1986. He died in 1987.

INTERNATIONAL

ALSO BY JAMES BALDWIN

JAMES BALDWIN

The Devil Finds Work

An Essay

VINTAGE INTERNATIONAL
Vintage Books
A Division of Random House, Inc.
New York

FIRST VINTAGE INTERNATIONAL EDITION,
SEPTEMBER 2011

Copyright © 1976 by James Baldwin

Vintage is a registered trademark and Vintage International and
colophon are trademarks of Random House, Inc.

Grateful acknowledgment is made to the following for permission to
reprint previously published material:
Alfred Music Publishing Co. Inc. and Hal Leonard Corporation:
Lyrics from "The Man That Got Away" from the motion picture *A Star Is Born*,
lyrics by Ira Gershwin, music by Harold Arlen, copyright © 1954 (Renewed) by
Harwin Music Co. and Ira Gershwin Music. All rights on behalf of Ira Gershwin
Music administered by WB Music Corp. All rights reserved. Reprinted by
permission of Alfred Music Publishing Co. Inc. and Hal Leonard Corporation.
Countdown Media: Lyrics from "Sing Sing Blues" by Joseph Kuhn.
Reprinted by permission of Countdown Media.

The Library of Congress has cataloged the Dial Press edition as follows:
Baldwin, James.
The devil finds work : an essay / by James Baldwin.
p. cm.
1. Baldwin, James, 1924–1987—Knowledge—Performing arts.
2. Motion picture plays, American—History and criticism.
3. African Americans in motion pictures.
PS3552.A45 Z515
791.43/09/73
76000028

Vintage ISBN: 978-0-307-27595-0

www.vintagebooks.com

Printed in the United States of America
11

For

PAULA-MARIA, on her birthday,
and JOHN LATHAM
and brother, DAVID MOSES

For our God is a consuming fire.

HEBREWS 12:29

The Devil Finds Work

ONE

Congo Square

Joan crawford's straight, narrow, and lonely back. We are following her through the corridors of a moving train. She is looking for someone, or she is trying to escape from someone. She is eventually intercepted by, I think, Clark Gable.

I am fascinated by the movement on, and of, the screen, that movement which is something like the heaving and swelling of the sea (though I have not yet been to the sea): and which is also something like the light which moves on, and especially beneath, the water.

I am about seven. I am with my mother, or my aunt. The movie is *Dance, Fools, Dance.*

I don't remember the film. A child is far too self-centered to relate to any dilemma which does not, somehow, relate to him— to his own evolving dilemma. The child escapes into what he would like his situation to be, and I certainly did not wish to be a fleeing fugitive on a moving train; and, also, with quite another part of my mind, I was aware that Joan Crawford was a white lady. Yet, I remember being sent to the store sometime later, and a colored woman, who, to me, looked exactly like Joan Crawford, was buying something. She was so incredibly beautiful—she seemed to be wearing the sunlight, rearranging it around her from time to time, with a movement of one hand, with a movement of her head, and with her smile—that, when she paid the man and started out of the store, I started out behind her. The storekeeper, who knew me, and others in the store who knew my mother's little boy (and who also knew my Miss Crawford!) laughed and called me back. Miss Crawford also laughed and looked down at me with so beautiful a smile that I was not even embarrassed. Which was rare for me.

Tom Mix, on his white horse. Actually, it was Tom Mix's hat, a shadow in the shadow of the hat, a kind of rocky background (which, again, was always moving) and the white horse. Tom Mix was a serial. Every Saturday, then, if memory serves, we left Tom Mix and some bleakly interchangeable girl in the most dreadful danger—or, rather, we left the hat and the shadow of the hat and the white horse: for the horse was not interchangeable and the serial could not have existed without it.

The Last of the Mohicans: Randolph Scott (a kind of fifteenth-rate Gary Cooper) and Binnie Barnes (a kind of funky Geraldine Fitzgerald), Heather Angel (a somewhat more bewildered Olivia de Havilland) and Philip Reed (a precursor of Anthony Quinn). Philip Reed was the Indian, Uncas, whose savage, not to say slavish adoration of Miss Angel's fine blonde frame drives her over a cliff, headlong, to her death. She has chosen death before dishonor, which made perfect sense. The erring Uncas eventually pays for his misguided lust with his life, and a tremulous, wet-eyed, brave couple, Randolph Scott and Binnie Barnes, eventually, hand in hand, manage to make it out of the wilderness. Into America, or back to England, I really do not remember, and I don't suppose that it matters.*

20,000 Years in Sing Sing: Spencer Tracy and Bette Davis. By this time, I had been taken in hand by a young white schoolteacher, a beautiful woman, very important to me. I was between ten and eleven. She had directed my first play and endured my first theatrical tantrums and had then decided to escort me into the world. She gave me books to read and talked to me about the books, and about the world: about Spain, for example, and Ethiopia, and Italy, and the German Third Reich; and took me to see plays and films, plays and films to which no one else would have dreamed of taking a ten-year-old boy. I loved her, of course, and absolutely, with a child's love; didn't understand half of what she said, but remembered it; and it stood me in good stead later. It is certainly partly because of her, who arrived in my terrifying life so soon, that I never really managed to hate white people—though, God knows, I have often wished to murder more than one or two. But Bill Miller—her name was Orilla, we called her Bill—was not white for me in the way, for example, that Joan Crawford was white, in the way that the landlords and the storekeepers and the cops and most of my teachers were white. She didn't baffle me that way and she never frightened me and she

---

* The novel, which I read much later, is not my favorite novel, and, on some other day, I may detail my quarrel with it; but it is far more honest and courageous than the film.

never lied to me. I never felt her pity, either, in spite of the fact that she sometimes brought us old clothes (because she worried about our winters) and cod-liver oil, especially for me, because I seemed destined, then, to be carried away by whooping cough.

I was a child, of course, and, therefore, unsophisticated. I don't seem ever to have had any innate need (or, indeed, any innate ability) to distrust people: and so I took Bill Miller as she was, or as she appeared to be to me. Yet, the difference between Miss Miller and other white people, white people as they lived in my imagination, and also as they were in life, had to have had a profound and bewildering effect on my mind. Bill Miller was not at all like the cops who had already beaten me up, she was not like the landlords who called me nigger, she was not like the storekeepers who laughed at me. I had found white people to be unutterably menacing, terrifying, mysterious—wicked: and they were mysterious, in fact, to the extent that they were wicked: the unfathomable question being, precisely, this one: what, under heaven, or beneath the sea, or in the catacombs of hell, could cause any people to act as white people acted? From Miss Miller, therefore, I began to suspect that white people did not act as they did because they were white, but for some other reason, and I began to try to locate and understand the reason. She, too, anyway, was treated like a nigger, especially by the cops, and she had no love for landlords.

My father said, during all the years I lived with him, that I was the ugliest boy he had ever seen, and I had absolutely no reason to doubt him. But it was not my father's hatred of *my* frog-eyes which hurt me, this hatred proving, in time, to be rather more resounding than real: I have my mother's eyes. When my father called me ugly, he was not attacking me so much as he was attacking my mother. (No doubt, he was also attacking my real, and unknown, father.) And I loved my mother. I knew that she loved me, and I sensed that she was paying an enormous price for me. I was a boy, and so I didn't really too much care that my father thought me hideous. (So I said to myself—this judgment, nevertheless, was to have a decidedly terrifying effect on my life.) But I thought that he must have been stricken blind (or was as mysteriously wicked as white people, a paralyzing thought) if he was unable to see that my mother was absolutely beyond any question the most beautiful woman in the world.

So, here, now, was Bette Davis, on that Saturday afternoon, in close-up, over a champagne glass, pop-eyes popping. I was astounded. I had caught my father, not in a lie, but in an infirmity. For, here, before me, after all, was a *movie star: white:* and if she was white and a movie star, she was *rich:* and she was *ugly.* I felt exactly the same way I felt, just before this moment, or just after, when I was in the street, playing, and I saw an old, very black, and very drunk woman stumbling up the sidewalk, and I ran upstairs to make my mother come to the window and see what I had found: *You see? You see? She's uglier than you, Mama! She's uglier than me!* Out of bewilderment, out of loyalty to my mother, probably, and also because I sensed something menacing and unhealthy (for me, certainly) in the face on the screen, I gave Davis's skin the dead-white greenish cast of something crawling from under a rock, but I was held, just the same, by the tense intelligence of the forehead, the disaster of the lips: and when she moved, she moved just like a nigger. Eventually, from a hospital bed, she murders someone, and Tracy takes the weight, to Sing Sing. In his arms, Davis cries and cries, and the movie ends. "What's going to happen to her now?" I asked Bill Miller. "We don't know," said Bill, conveying to me, nevertheless, that she would probably never get over it, that people pay for what they do.

I had not yet heard Bessie Smith's *"why they call this place the Sing Sing?/Come stand here by this rock pile, and listen to these hammers ring,"* and it would be seven years before I would begin working on the railroad. It was to take a longer time than that before I would cry; a longer time than that before I would cry in anyone's arms; and a long long long long time before I would begin to realize what I myself was doing with my enormous eyes—or vice versa. This had nothing to do with Davis, the actress, or with all those hang-ups I didn't yet know I had: I had discovered that my infirmity might not be my doom; my infirmity, or infirmities, might be forged into weapons.

For, I was not only considered by my father to be ugly. I was considered by everyone to be "strange," including my poor mother, who didn't, however, beat me for it. Well, if I was "strange"—and I knew that I must be, otherwise people would not have treated me so strangely, and I would not have been so miserable—perhaps I could find a way to use my strangeness. A "strange" child, anyway, dimly and fearfully apprehends that the years are not likely to make him less strange. Therefore, if he wishes to live, he must calculate, and I knew that I had to live. I very much wanted my mother to be happy and to be proud of me, and I very much loved my brothers and my sisters, who, in a sense, were all I had. My father showed no favoritism, he did not beat me worse than the others because I was not his son. (I didn't know this then, anyway, none of the children did, and by the time we all found out, it became just one more detail of the peculiar journey we had made in company with each other.) I knew, too, that my mother depended on me. I was not always dependable, for no child can be, but I tried: and I knew that I might have to prepare myself to be, one day, the actual head of my family. I did not actually do this, either, for we were all forced to take on our responsibilities each for the other, and to discharge them in our different ways. The eldest can be, God knows, as much a burden as a help, and is doomed to be something of a mystery for those growing up behind him—a mystery when not, indeed, an intolerable exasperation. *I,* nevertheless, was the eldest, a responsibility I did not intend to fail, and my first conscious calculation as to how to go about defeating the world's intentions for me and mine began on that Saturday afternoon in what we called *the movies,* but which was actually my first entrance into the cinema of my mind.

I read *Uncle Tom's Cabin* over and over and over again—this is the first book I can remember having read—and then I read *A Tale of Two Cities*—over and over and over again. Bill Miller takes me to see *A Tale of Two Cities,* at the Lincoln, on 135th Street. I am twelve.

I did not yet know that virtually every black community in America contains a movie house, or, sometimes, in those days, an actual theater, called the Lincoln, or the Booker T. Washington, nor did I know why; any more than I knew why The Cotton Club was called The Cotton Club. I knew about Lincoln only that he had freed the slaves (in the South, which made the venture remote from me) and then had been shot, dead, in a theater, by an actor; and a movie I was never to see, called *The Prisoner of Shark Island,* had something to do with the murder of Lincoln. How I knew this, I do not remember precisely. But I know that I read everything I could get my hands on, including movie advertisements, and *Uncle Tom's Cabin* had had a tremendous impact on me, and I certainly reacted to the brutal conjunction of the words, *prisoner,* and *shark,* and *island.* I may have feared becoming a prisoner, or feared that I was one already; had never seen a shark—I hoped: but I was certainly trapped on an island. And, in any case, the star of this film, Warner Baxter, later, but during the same era, made a film with the female star of *A Tale of Two Cities,* called *Slave Ship:* which I did not see, either.

I knew about Booker T. Washington less than I knew about my father's mother, who had been born a slave, and who died in our house when I was little: a child cannot make the connection between *slave* and *grandmother,* and it was to take me a while (mainly because I had discovered the Schomburg collection at the 135th Street Library) to read *Up From Slavery:* but, when I read it, I no longer knew which way was up. As for The Cotton Club, I knew only that it was a dance hall which gave out free Thanksgiving dinners every Thanksgiving (!) for which my brother, George, and I, stood in line. Which means that I knew that I was poor, and knew that I was black, but did not yet know what being black really meant, what it meant, that is, in the history of my country, and in my own history. Bill could instruct me as to how poverty came about and what it meant and what it did, and, also, what it was meant to do: but she could not instruct me as to blackness, except obliquely, feeling that she had neither the right nor the authority, and also knowing that I was certain to find out. Thus, she tried to suggest to me the extent to which the world's social and economic arrangements are responsible for (and to) the world's victims. But a victim may or may not have a color, just as he may or may not have virtue: a difficult, not to say unpopular notion, for nearly everyone prefers to be defined by his status, which, unlike his virtue, is ready to wear.

The 1936 Metro-Goldwyn-Mayer production of *A Tale of Two Cities* ends with this enormity sprawled across the screen:

I am the resurrection and the life, saith the Lord: he that believeth in me, though he were dead, yet shall he live; and he that believeth in me shall never die.

I had lived with this text all my life, which made encountering it on the screen of the Lincoln Theater absolutely astounding: and I had lived with the people of *A Tale of Two Cities* for very nearly as long. I had no idea what *Two Cities* was really about, any more than I knew what *Uncle Tom's Cabin* was really about, which was why I had read them both so obsessively: they had something to tell me. It was this particular child's way of circling around the question of what it meant to be a nigger. It was the reason that I was reading Dostoevsky, a writer—or, rather, for me, a messenger—whom I would have had to understand, obviously, even less: my relentless pursuit of *Crime and Punishment* made my father (vocally) and my mother (silently) consider the possibility of brain fever. I was intrigued, but not misled, by the surface of these novels—Sydney Carton's noble renunciation of his life on the spectacular guillotine, Tom's forbearance before Simon Legree, the tracking down of Raskolnikov: the time of my time was to reduce all these images to the angel dancing on the edge of the junkie's needle: I did not believe in any of these people so much as I believed in their situation, which I suspected, dreadfully, to have something to do with my own.

And it had clearly escaped everyone's notice that I had already been bull-whipped through the Psalms of David and The Book of Job, to say nothing of the arrogant and loving Isaiah, the doomed Ezekiel, and the helplessly paranoiac Saint Paul: such a forced march, designed to prepare the mind for conciliation and safety, can also prepare it for subversion and danger. For, I was on Job's side, for example, *though He slay me, yet will I trust Him, and I will maintain mine own ways before Him*—You will not talk to *me* from the safety of your whirlwind, never—and, yet, something in me, out of the unbelievable pride and sorrow and beauty of my father's face, caused me to understand—I did not understand, perhaps I still do not understand, and never will, caused me to begin to accept the fatality and the inexorability of that voice out of the whirlwind, for if one is not able to live with so crushing and continuing a mystery, one is not able to live.

The pride and sorrow and beauty of my father's face: for that man I called my father really *was* my father in every sense except the biological, or literal one. He formed me, and he raised me, and he did not let me starve: and he gave me something, however harshly, and however little I wanted it, which prepared me for an impending horror which he could not prevent. This is not a Western idea, but fathers and sons arrive at that relationship only by claiming that relationship: that is, by paying for it. If the relationship of father to son could really be reduced to biology, the whole earth would blaze with the glory of fathers and sons. (But to pursue this further carries us far beyond the confines of the present discussion.)

In the novel, *A Tale of Two Cities,* it had been Madame Defarge who most struck me. I recognized that unrelenting hatred, for it was all up and down my streets, and in my father's face and voice. The wine cask, *shattered like a walnut shell,* shattered every Saturday night on the corner of our street, and, yes, Dickens was right, the gutters turned a bright and then a rusty red. I understood the knitted registers as hope and fate, for I knew that everything (including my own name) had long been written in

The Book: *you may run on a great long time but great God Almighty's going to cut you down!* I understood the meaning of the rose in the turban of Madame Defarge as she sits knitting in the wine shop, the flower in the headdress meant to alert the neighborhood to the presence of a spy. We lived by such signals, and long before it was safe to say *there is a rose in Spanish Harlem!*

When, at last, in the film, the people rise and fill the streets and alleys and hurl themselves onto the drawbridge of the Bastille, I was tremendously stirred and frightened. I did not really know who these people were, or why they were in the streets—they were white: and a white mob can be in no way reassuring to a black boy (even though, or if, he cannot say why). If, in the novel, it was Madame Defarge who most held me, in the film two images and one moment stand out, even from this distance. The first is a long climb up an outside staircase, in Paris, when Lucie Manette and Dr. Lorry and Ernest Defarge go to retrieve Lucie's father, Dr. Manette: for I knew about staircases. The second is when the carriage of the Marquis races headlong through a provincial village. We are confronted with the speeding wheels of the carriage, the relentless hooves of the horses, and a small, running, ragged boy, trying to get out of the way. He is knocked down, he is run over, he is killed; and I knew something about that. The moment that most stands out, for me, is that moment in the tumbril, near the end of the film, when the seamstress (Isabel Jewell) recognizes that Sydney Carton (Ronald Colman) is dying in his friend's stead. I knew nothing about *that,* but I had been taught *greater love hath no man than this,* and something in me believed it. Yet, when Bill whispered to me, during the scene of the storming of the Bastille, "Every time somebody drops from the drawbridge, they die," though I watched the people dropping off the drawbridge like so many dead cockroaches being swept into the dust pan, I was also aware that Bill was not telling me that Metro-Goldwyn-Mayer was murdering all these people, any more than that that guillotine was really going to chop off Ronald Colman's head. The guillotine was going to chop off *Sydney Carton's* head: my first director was instructing me in the discipline and power of make-believe.

For, while believing it all, and *really* believing it, I still knew that Madame Defarge was really an actress named Blanche Yurka, and that Lucie Manette was really an English girl, named Elizabeth Allan. Something implacable in the set of Yurka's mouth probably reminded me of my grandmother, and I knew that Elizabeth Allan-Lucie Manette reminded me of my music teacher, a Miss Taub, with whom I was desperately in love. When Lucie Manette and Charles Darnay are torn from each other's arms in the courtroom, tears rose to my eyes, for I knew something about *that:* yet, at the very same time, I also knew that Charles Darnay was really an actor, named Donald Woods. This was the first time in my life, after all, that I had seen a *screen rendition* (so the ads and the press put it) of a novel, which, considering my age, I could claim to know. And I felt very close to the actors, who had not betrayed the friends I had lived with for nearly as long as I had lived with the people of *Uncle Tom's Cabin.*

I had read *Uncle Tom's Cabin* compulsively, the book in one hand, the newest baby on my hipbone. I was trying to find out something, sensing something in the book of some immense import for me: which, however, I knew I did not really understand.

My mother got scared. She hid the book. The last time she hid it, she hid it on the highest shelf above the bathtub. I was somewhere around seven or eight. God knows how I did it, but I somehow climbed up and dragged the book down. Then, my mother, as she herself puts it, "didn't hide it anymore," and, indeed, from that moment, though in fear and trembling, began to let me go.

I understood, as Bill had intended me to, something of revolution—understood, that is, something of the universal and inevitable human ferment which explodes into what is called a revolution. *Revolution:* the word had a solemn, dreadful ring: what was going on in Spain was a *revolution.* Revolution was the only hope of the American working class—the *proletariat:* and world-wide revolution was the only hope of the world. I could understand (or, rather, accept) all this, as it were, negatively. I could not see where I fit in this formulation, and I did not see where blacks fit. I don't think that I ever dared pose this question to Bill, partly because I hadn't yet really accepted, or understood, that *I* was black and also because I knew (and didn't want her to know, although, of course, she did) how much my father distrusted and disliked her. My father was certainly a proletarian, but I had been sent downtown often to pay his union dues, and I knew how much he hated these greasy, slimy men—also proletarians—whom he called, quite rightly, robbers.

In the film, I was not overwhelmed by the guillotine. The guillotine had been very present for me in the novel because I already wanted, and for very good reasons, to lop off heads. But: once begun, how to distinguish one head from another, and how, where, and for what reason, would the process stop? Beneath the resonance of the word, *revolution,* thundered the word, *revenge.* But: *vengeance is mine, saith the Lord:* a hard saying, the identity of *the Lord* becoming, with the passage of time, either a private agony or an abstract question. And, to put it as simply as it can be put, unless one can conceive of (and endure) an abstract life, there can be no abstract questions. A question is a threat, the door which slams shut, or swings open: on another threat.

I was haunted, for example, by Alexandre Manette's document, in *A Tale of Two Cities,* describing the murder of a peasant boy—who, dying, speaks: *I say, we were so robbed, and hunted, and were made so poor, that our father told us it was a dreadful thing to bring a child into this world, and that what we should most pray for was that our women might be barren and our miserable race die out! (I had never before,* observes Dr. Manette, *seen the sense of being oppressed, bursting forth like a fire.)*

Dickens has not seen it at all. The wretched of the earth do not decide to become extinct, they resolve, on the contrary, to multiply: life is their only weapon against life, life is all that they have. This is why the dispossessed and starving will never be convinced (though some may be coerced) by the population-control programs of the civilized. I have watched the dispossessed and starving laboring in the fields which others own, with their transistor radios at their ear, all day long: so they learn, for example, along with equally weighty matters, that the Pope, one of the heads of the civilized world, forbids to the civilized that abortion which is being, literally, forced on them, the wretched. The civilized have created the wretched, quite coldly and deliberately, and do not intend to change the *status quo;* are responsible for their slaughter and enslavement; rain down bombs on defenseless children whenever and wherever they decide that their "vital interests" are menaced, and think nothing of torturing a man to death: these people are not to be taken seriously when they speak of the "sanctity" of human life, or the "conscience" of the civilized world. There is a "sanctity" involved with bringing a child into this world: it is better than bombing one out of it. Dreadful indeed it is to see a starving child, but the answer to that is not to prevent the child's arrival but to restructure the world so that the child can live in it: so that the "vital interest" of the world becomes nothing less than the life of the child. However—I would not have said any of this then, nor is so absurd a notion about to engulf the world now. But we were all starving children, after all, and none of our fathers, even at their most embittered and enraged, had ever suggested that we "die out." It was not *we* who were supposed to *die out:* this was, of all notions, the most forbidden, and we learned this from the cradle. Every trial, every beating, every drop of blood, every tear, were meant to be used by us for a day that was coming—for a day that was certainly coming, absolutely certainly, certainly coming: not for us, perhaps, but for our children. The children of the despised and rejected are menaced from the moment they stir in the womb, and are therefore sacred in a way that the children of the saved are not. And the children know it, which is how they manage to raise their children, and why they will not be persuaded—by their children's murderers, after all—to cease having children.

But I was haunted, too, by the fact that it is Dr. Manette's testimony, written in prison, and recuperated by Ernest Defarge upon the storming of the Bastille, which dooms his son-in-law to death. The Defarges seize and hide this document in order to use it against the son-in-law at the latter's trial: at which trial, Dr. Manette is chief witness for the defense—or, in other words, in fact, his son-in-law's only hope.

Manette wrote his testimony in agony and silence, never expecting to see his daughter again, and unable, of course, to imagine that his daughter would marry one of the descendants of the house which had condemned him to a living death. His testimony ends: *them and their descendants, to the last of their race, I . . . denounce them to Heaven and to earth.* His son-in-law is the descendant of the "race" which had imprisoned him, and the "last" of that race, denounced by him, is flesh of his flesh, his granddaughter. Which connected for me, horribly, with the testimony of Madame Defarge, sister of the murdered boy: *that brother was my brother, that father was my father, those dead are my dead and that summons to answer for all those things descends to me!* Her husband reluctantly agrees that this is so, whereupon Madame Defarge says, *Then tell wind and fire where to stop, but don't tell me!*

I understood *that:* I had seen it in the face, heard it in the voice of many a black man or woman, sweeping the pavement, wrestling with the garbage cans, men and women whose children were dying faster than those MGM extras dropping from the drawbridge. *If I love you, I love you, and I don't give a damn. You my nigger, nigger, if you don't get no bigger. I will cut your dick off, I will cut your balls out. I ain't got to do nothing but stay black and die and I'm black already! Honey. Don't be like that. Honey. Don't do me like that. We in this shit together, and you need me and I need you, now ain't that so? Who going to take care of us if we don't take care of each other?*

I feared, feared—like a thief in the night, as one of my brothers would put it—to connect all this with my father and mother and everyone I knew, and with myself, and to connect all this with black Uncle Tom: no more than I had wished to be that fleeing fugitive on that moving train did I desire to endure his destiny or meet his end. Uncle Tom really believed *vengeance is mine, saith the Lord,* for he believed in the Lord, as I flattered myself I did not: this inconvenient faith (described, furthermore, by a white woman) obscured the fact that Tom allowed himself to be murdered for refusing to disclose the road taken by the runaway slave. Because Uncle Tom would not take vengeance into his own hands, he was not a hero for me. Heroes, as far as I could then see, were white, and not merely because of the movies but because of the land in which I lived, of which movies were simply a reflection: I despised and feared those heroes because they *did* take vengeance into their own hands. They thought that vengeance was theirs to take. This difficult coin did not cease to spin, it had neither heads nor tails: for what white people took into their hands could scarcely even be called vengeance, it was something less and something more. The Scottsboro boys, for example—for the Scottsboro Case has begun—were certainly innocent of anything requiring vengeance. My father's youngest son by his first marriage, nine years older than I, who had vanished from our lives, might have been one of those boys, now being murdered by my fellow Americans on the basis of the rape charge delivered by two white whores: and I was reading Angelo Herndon's *Let Me Live*. Yes. I understood *that:* my countrymen were my enemy, and I had already begun to hate them from the bottom of my heart.

Angelo Herndon was a young, black labor organizer in the Deep South, railroaded to prison, who lived long enough, at least, to write a book about it—the George Jackson of the era. No one resembling him, or anyone resembling any of the Scottsboro Boys, nor anyone resembling my father, has yet made an appearance on the American cinema scene. Perhaps to compensate for this, Bill now takes me to See Sylvia Sidney and Henry Fonda in the Walter Wanger production of Fritz Lang's *You Only Live*

Once. I, also, either with her or without her, I don't remember, see the Warner Brothers production (or *screen rendition,* which pompous formulation I adored) of a novel I had read, Ward Greene's *Death in the Deep South,* brought to the screen by (I think) Mervyn LeRoy, as *They Won't Forget,* starring Claude Rains; and Samuel Goldwyn's production of William Wyler's *Dead End,* again starring Sylvia Sidney. Who also starred in the film version of a play Bill took me to see, the WPA Living News-paper production,—*one third of a nation*—.

It is not entirely true that no one from the world I knew had yet made an appearance on the American screen: there were, for ex-ample, Stepin Fetchit and Willie Best and Manton Moreland, all of whom, rightly or wrongly, I loathed. It seemed to me that they lied about the world I knew, and debased it, and certainly I did not know anybody like them—as far as I could tell; for it is also possible that their comic, bug-eyed terror contained the truth concerning a terror by which I hoped never to be engulfed.

Yet, I had no reservations at all concerning the terror of the black janitor in *They Won't Forget.* I think that it was a black actor named Clinton Rosewood who played this part, and he looked a little like my father. He is terrified because a young white girl, in this small Southern town, has been raped and murdered, and her body has been found on the premises of which he is the janitor. (Lana Turner, in her first movie, is the raped and murdered girl, which is, perhaps, a somewhat curious beginning for so gold-plated a career.) The role of the janitor is small, yet the man's face hangs in my memory until today: and the film's icy brutality both scared me and strengthened me. The Southern politician (Rains) needs an issue on which to be re-elected. He decides, therefore, that to pin the rape and murder of the white girl on a black man is insufficiently sensational. He very coldly frames a white Northern schoolteacher for this crime, and brings about his death at the hands of a lynch mob. (And I knew that this was exactly what would have happened to Bill, if such a mob had ever got its hands on her.) Unlike the later *Ox-Bow Incident,* in which a similar lynching is partially redeemed by the reading of a letter, which, presumably, will cause the members of the mob to repent the horror of what they have done and resolve to become better men and women, and also unlike the later *Intruder in the Dust,* which suggests the same hopeful improbability, *They Won't Forget* ends with the teacher dead and the politician triumphantly re-elected. As he watches the widow walk down the courthouse steps, he mutters, seeming, almost, to stifle a yawn, *I wonder if he really did it, after all.*

And, yes: I was beginning to understand *that.*

Sylvia Sidney was the only American film actress who reminded me of a colored girl, or woman—which is to say that she was the only American film actress who reminded me of reality. All of the others, without exception, were white, and, even when they moved me (like Margaret Sullavan or Bette Davis or Carole Lombard) they moved me from that distance. Some instinct caused me profoundly to distrust the sense of life they projected: this sense of life could certainly never, in any case, be used by me, and, while *His* eye might be on the sparrow, mine had to be on the hawk. And, similarly, while I admired Edward G. Robinson and James Cagney (and, on a more demanding level, Fredric March), the only actor of the era with whom I identified was

Henry Fonda. I was not alone. A black friend of mine, after seeing Henry Fonda in *The Grapes of Wrath,* swore that Fonda had
colored blood. You could tell, he said, by the way Fonda walked
down the road at the end of the film: *white men don't walk like
that!* and he imitated Fonda's stubborn, patient, wide-legged hike
away from the camera. My reaction to Sylvia Sidney was certainly
due, in part, to the kind of film she appeared in during that era—
Fury; Mary Burns, Fugitive; You and Me; Street Scene (I was certain, even, that I knew the meaning of the title of a film she made
with Gene Raymond, which I never saw, *Behold My Wife).* It was
almost as though she and I had a secret: she seemed to know
something I knew. *Every street in New York ends in a river:* this is
the legend which begins the film, *Dead End,* and I was enor-
mously grateful for it. I had never thought of that before. Sylvia
Sidney, facing a cop in this film, pulling her black hat back from
her forehead: *One of you lousy cops gave me that.* She was always
being beaten up, victimized, weeping, and she should have been
drearier than Tom Mix's girl friends. But I always believed her—
in a way, she reminded me of Bill, for I had seen Bill facing hostile cops. Bill took us on a picnic downtown once, and there was
supposed to be ice cream waiting for us at a police station. The
cops didn't like Bill, didn't like the fact that we were colored kids,
and didn't want to give up the ice cream. I don't remember anything Bill said. I just remember her face as she stared at the cop,
clearly intending to stand there until the ice cream all over the
world melted or until the earth's surface froze, and she got us our
ice cream, saying *Thank you,* I remember, as we left. *You Only
Live Once* was the most powerful movie I had seen until that moment. The only other film to hit me as hard, at that time of my
life, was *The Childhood of Maxim Gorky,* which, for me, had not

been about white people. Similarly, while *20,000 Years in Sing Sing* had concerned the trials of a finally somewhat improbable white couple, *You Only Live Once* came much much closer to home.

It is the top of 1937. I am not yet thirteen.

Fury, MGM, 1936, is, I believe, Lang's first American film. It is meant to be a study of mob violence, on which level it is indignant, sincere, and inept. Since the mob separates the lovers almost at the beginning of the film, the film works as a love story only intermittently, and to the extent that one responds to the lovers (Sylvia Sidney and Spencer Tracy). It is an exceedingly uneasy and uneven film, with both the lovers and the mob placed, really, in the German Third Reich, which Lang has not so much fled as furiously repudiated, and to which he is still reacting. (The railroad station at which the lovers separate is heavy with menace, and the train which carries Sidney away to go to work in another town is rather like the train to a bloody destination unknown.) Lang's is the *fury* of the film: but his grasp of the texture of American life is still extremely weak: he has not yet really left Germany. His fury, nevertheless, manages to convey something of the idle, aimless, compulsive wickedness of idle, terrified, aimless people, who can come together only as a mob: but his hatred of these people also makes them, at least, unreal. God knows what Lang had already seen, in Germany.

By the time of *You Only Live Once*, Lang had found his American feet. He never succeeded quite so brilliantly again. Considering the speed with which we moved from the New Deal to World War II, to Yalta, to the Marshall Plan, the Truman Doctrine, to

Korea, and the House Un-American Activities Committee, this may not be his fault.

(One of the last of his films, entitled *Beyond a Reasonable Doubt*, starring Joan Fontaine, Dana Andrews, and Sydney Blackmer, is an utterly shameless apology for American justice, the work of a defeated man. But, children, yes, it be's that way sometimes.)

Lang's concern, or obsession, was with the fact and the effect of human loneliness, and the ways in which we are all responsible for the creation, and the fate, of the isolated monster: whom we isolate because we recognize him as living within us. This is what his great German film, *M*, which launched Peter Lorre, is all about. In the American context, there being no way for him to get to the *nigger*, he could use only that other American prototype, the criminal, *le gangster*. The premise of *You Only Live Once* is that Eddie Taylor (Henry Fonda) is an ex-convict who wants to go "straight": but the society will not allow him to live down, or redeem, his criminal past. This apparently banal situation is thrust upon us with so heavy a hand that one is forced—as I was, even so long ago—to wonder if one is resisting the film or resisting the truth. But, however one may wish to defend oneself against Lang's indictment of the small, faceless people, always available for any public ceremony and absent forever from any private one, who *are* society, one is left defenseless before his study of the result, which is the isolation and the doom of the lovers.

Very early in the film we meet the earnest and popular prison chaplain—a priest: we meet him as he pitches the ball to the men who are playing baseball in the prison courtyard. It is a curiously loaded moment, a disturbing image: perhaps only an exiled German, at that period of our history, would have dreamed of so connecting games and slaughter, thus foreshadowing the fate of the accomplice, who is, in this case, the priest. The film does not suggest that the priest's popularity has anything to do with the religious instruction he, presumably, brings to the men—his popularity is due to his personal qualities, which include a somewhat overworked cheerfulness: and his function, at bottom, is to prepare the men for death. His role, also, is to make the prison more bearable, both for the men in the courtyard and the guard behind the machine gun in the tower. And he is, also, of course, to prepare these men for their eventual freedom beyond these walls—which freedom, according to Lang's savage and elaborately articulated vision, does not and probably cannot exist.

The film has a kind of claustrophobic physicality—Sidney is first seen, for example, behind a desk, trapped, and Lang forces us to concentrate on her maneuvers to free herself, smiling all the way. (She's trapped behind her desk by a telephone and an apple vendor who has come to City Hall, where Sidney works, to complain that policemen eat his apples for free.) The first reunion of the lovers takes place with bars between them: it takes a moment before they realize that the gate is open, the man is being set free. There is a marvelous small moment in the flop house, with Fonda pacing the room the way he paced the cell, and pausing at the window to listen to the Salvation Army Band outside, singing, *if you love your mother, meet her in the skies.* I cannot imagine any native-born white American daring to use, so laconically, a banality so nearly comic in order to capture so deep a distress.

The genuine indignation which informs this film is a quality which was very shortly to disappear out of the American cinema, and severely to be menaced in American life. In a way, we were all niggers in the thirties. I do not know if that really made us more friendly with each other—at bottom, I doubt that, for more would remain of that friendliness today—but it was harder then, and riskier, to attempt a separate peace, and benign neglect was not among our possibilities. The Okies, of *The Grapes of Wrath,* were still crossing the plains in their jalopy and had not yet arrived in California, there, every single one of them, to encounter running water, and to become cops. Neither Steinbeck nor Dos Passos had yet said, *my country, right or wrong,* nor did anyone suppose that they ever could—but they did; and Hemingway was as vocal concerning the Spanish revolution as he was to be silent concerning the Cuban one.

There is that moment in the film, in prison, when Fonda whispers to Sidney, through jailhouse glass, *Get me a gun.* Sidney said, *I can't get you a gun. You'll kill somebody!* and Fonda says, *What do you think they're going to do to me?*

I understood *that:* it was a real question. I was living with that question.

It is the priest who covers for the trapped and weary girl when she attempts to smuggle a gun into the prison, and it is the priest whom Fonda murders, with a gun. And I wondered about that, the well-meaning accomplice and his fate: he is murdered because Fonda does not believe him, even though he is, in fact, speaking the truth. But the prisoner has no way of knowing with whom the priest is playing ball at the moment and so dares not risk believing him. This dread is underscored by the film's last line, delivered (in the dying prisoner's memory) by the priest: *the gates are open.* I knew damn well that the gates were *not* open, and, by this time, in any case, the lovers were dead.

———

Dead End, on the other hand, left me cold, and so did *Street Scene*, for the same reason: my streets were funkier and more dangerous than that. I had seen the gangster, Baby-Face Martin (Humphrey Bogart), in *my* streets, with his one-hundred-dollar suits, and his silk shirts, and his hat: sometimes he was a pimp and sometimes he was a preacher and often he was both: but Baby-Face always had the same taste in women, boys, and cars. I knew no one like the heroine, Drina (Sylvia Sidney), except certain high-yellow bitches, whose concern for their younger brother, if they had any concern, would long before have forced them to hit the block, hit the road, or hit a clean old banker, and steal the keys to the long old highway; or, in other words, the severity of the social situation which *Dead End* so romanticizes (somewhat like its direct descendant, *West Side Story)* utterly precludes the innocence of its heroine. Much closer to the truth are the gangster, his broken mother, and his broken girl—yes: I had seen *that*. The script is unable to face the fact that it is merely another version of that brutal fantasy known as the American success story: this helpless dishonesty is revealed by the script's resolution. I was by no means certain that I approved of the hero's decision to inform on Baby-Face, to turn him over to the police, and bring about his death. In my streets, we never called the cops, and whoever turned anyone in to the cops was a pariah. I did not believe, though the film insists on it, that the hero (Joel McCrea) turned in the gangster in order to save the children. I had never seen any children saved that way. In my own experience, on the contrary, and not only because I was watching Bill, I had observed that those who really wished to save the children became themselves, immediately, the target of the police. I could believe—though the film pretends that this consideration never entered the hero's mind—that the hero turned in the gangster in order to collect the reward money: that reward money which will allow the hero and heroine to escape from the stink of the children: for I had certainly seen attempts at *that*. Should the hero and heroine take the younger brother with them into that so celebrated American mainstream, the boy, having no friends, and finding, therefore, no resonance, no corroboration of himself anywhere, will become either a derelict, or the most monstrous of patriots. Or, perhaps (trying to escape and atone, or, perhaps, simply trying to live) the boy will become a kind of revolutionary, a superior and dedicated gangster: for there is a reason that the heroes of the poor resemble so little (and yet so closely resemble!) the heroes of the rich. I do not wish to be misunderstood as suggesting, for example, that the late Adam Clayton Powell was in any way whatever a bandit, but that is what the white world called him. Harlem's position, therefore, as concerned Adam, was that Adam might have his faults, but that he was certainly a better man than any of his accusers, his accusers being on our backs: and that is why Harlem never abandoned him. Of course, I could not have said any of that then, either. I knew about Adam only that he was the son of "old" Adam, the pastor of Abyssinian Baptist Church, of which church we had been members when I was little; and that he had been instrumental, in the wake of the 1935 Harlem riot, in getting black people hired—for the first time—in the stores on 125th Street where we spent so much of our money—the word, "money," here being meant to convey the image of black fistfuls of nickels and dimes.

In any case, the happy resolution of *Dead End* could mean nothing to me, since, even with some money, black people could move only into black neighborhoods: which is not to be interpreted as meaning that we wished to move into white neighborhoods. We wished, merely, to be free to move. At the time that I am speaking of we had not yet even begun to move across the river, into the Bronx.

Bill takes me to see my first play, the Orson Welles production of *Macbeth*, with an all-black cast, at the Lafayette Theater, on 132nd Street and Seventh Avenue, in Harlem.

I do not remember if I had already read *Macbeth*. My impression is that I read the play when Bill told me she was taking me to see it. In any case, before the curtain rose, I knew the play by heart.

I don't think that the name, *Shakespeare*, meant very much to me in those years. I was not yet intimidated by the name—that was to come later. I had read a play which took place in Scotland. Bill had not warned me—she may not have known—that Welles had transposed the play to Haiti.

I am still about twelve or thirteen. I can be fairly certain about all this, because my life changed so violently when I entered the church, and I entered the church around the time of fourteen. When I entered the church, I ceased going to the theater. It took me awhile to realize that I was working in one.

There is an enormous difference because the first time I ever really saw black actors at work was on the stage: and it is important to emphasize that the people I was watching were black, like me. Nothing that I had seen before had prepared me for this— which is a melancholy comment indeed, but I cannot be blamed for an ignorance which an entire republic had deliberately inculcated.

The distance between oneself—the audience—and a screen

performer is an absolute: a paradoxical absolute, masquerading as intimacy. No one, for example, will ever really know whether Katharine Hepburn or Bette Davis or Humphrey Bogart or Spencer Tracy or Clark Gable—or John Wayne—can, or could, really act, or not, nor does anyone care: acting is not what they are required to do. Their acting ability, so far from being what attracts their audience, can often be what drives their audience away. One does not go to see them act: one goes to watch them *be*. One does not go to see Humphrey Bogart, *as Sam Spade:* one goes to see Sam Spade, *as Humphrey Bogart.* I don't wish, here, to belabor a point to which we shall, presently, and somewhat elaborately, be compelled to return: but, *no one,* I read somewhere, a long time ago, *makes his escape personality black.* That the movie star is an "escape" personality indicates one of the irreducible dangers to which the moviegoer is exposed: the danger of surrendering to the corroboration of one's fantasies as they are thrown back from the screen. The danger is as great for the performer: Bette Davis may have longed, all these years, to play Mrs. Alving, in *Ghosts,* and Spencer Tracy may have carried with him to the grave an unfulfilled *King Lear*—nobody was about to let them try it, for fear that their public would feel themselves betrayed, This is one of the reasons that Joan Crawford, for example, doesn't like the film *Rain,* in which she starred. God knows that it's not a very good picture, but Crawford didn't write the abysmal script. She made the mistake, and very honorably, after all, of trying to be Miss Sadie Thompson instead of Miss Joan Crawford, and the kids didn't like that at all.

For the tension in the theater is a very different, and very particular tension: this tension between the real and the imagined *is* the theater, and this is why the theater will always remain a necessity. One is not in the presence of shadows, but responding to one's flesh and blood: in the theater, we are re-creating each other. Clearly, now, when speaking of the theater, I am not referring to those desperate and debilitating commercial ventures on which Broadway embarks each season, or those grim "revivals" of stillborn plays of which London is so fond, or those "adaptations" of American monstrosities which have been the rage of Paris for so long. Nor, in the present instance, is the term, "one's flesh and blood" meant to refer, merely, to the spectacle of a black boy seeing, for the first time in his life, living black actors on a living stage: we are *all* each other's flesh and blood.

This is the truth which it is very difficult for the theater to deny, and when it attempts to do so the same thing happens to the theater as happens to the church: it becomes sterile and irrelevant, a blasphemy, and the true believer goes elsewhere—carrying, as it happens, the church and the theater with him, and leaving the form behind. For, the church and the theater are carried within us and it is we who create them, out of our need and out of an impulse more mysterious than our desire. If this seems to be saying that the life of the theater and the life of the church are dependent on maverick freak poets and visionaries, I can only point out that these difficult creatures are *also* our flesh and blood, and are also created by our need and out of an impulse more mysterious than our desire.

In the darkened Lafayette Theater—that moment when the house lights dim in the theater is not at all like the dimming of the house lights in the movies—I watched the narrow, horizontal ribbon of light which connects the stage curtain to the floor of the stage, and which also separates them. That narrow ribbon of light then contains a mystery. That mystery may contain the future—you are, yourself, suspended as mortal as that ribbon. No one can possibly know what is about to happen: it is happening, each time, for the first time, for the only time. For this reason, although I did not know this, I had never before, in the movies, been aware of the audience: in the movies, we knew what was going to happen, and, if we wanted to, we could stay there all afternoon, seeing it happen over and over again.

But I was aware of the audience now. Everyone seemed to be waiting, as I was waiting. The curtain rose.

Between three and four years later, that is, around the time that I was seventeen, my best friend, Emile, took me to a movie at the Irving Place Theater, a Russian movie, since America and Russia were allies then. My friend is a Jew—an American Jew, of Spanish descent: he was then, and is today, one of the most honest and honorable people I have ever known. He took me to the movie because he was trying to help me leave the church. I had not been to a film, or a theater from the time of my conversion, which came hard upon the heels of *Macbeth*.

At this time of my life, Emile was the only friend I had who knew to what extent my ministry tormented me. I knew that I could not stay in the pulpit. I could not make my peace with that particular lie—a lie, in any case, for me. I did not want to become Baby-Face Martin—I could see that coming, and, indeed, it demanded no spectacular perception, since I found myself surrounded by what I was certain to become. But neither did I know how to leave—to jump: it could not be explained to my brothers and sisters, or my mother, and my father had begun his descent into the valley. Emile took me to this film, of which I remember only a close-up of a tambourine. I played the tambourine, in church: the tambourine on the screen might as well have been Gabriel's trumpet. I collapsed, weeping, terrified, and Emile led me out. He walked me up to Herald Square. It was night. He talked to me; he tried to make me see something—tried to do something only a friend can do: and challenged me, thus:

Even if what I was preaching was gospel, I had no right to preach it if I no longer believed it. To stay in the church merely because I was afraid of leaving it was unutterably far beneath me, and too despicable a cowardice for him to support in any friend of his. Therefore, on the coming Sunday, he would buy two tickets to a Broadway matinee and meet me on the steps of the 42nd Street Library, at two o'clock in the afternoon. He knew that I spent all day Sunday in church—the point, precisely, of the challenge. If I were not on the steps of the library (in the bookshelves of which so much of my trouble had begun!) then he would be ashamed of me and never speak to me again, and I would be ashamed of myself.

(I cannot resist observing that this still seems to me a quite extraordinary confrontation between two adolescents, one white and one black: but, then, I had never forgotten Bill's quiet statement, when I went down to her house on 12th Street to tell her that I had been "saved" and would not be going to the movies, or the theater anymore—which meant that I would not be seeing her anymore: *I've lost a lot of respect for you.* Perhaps, in the intervening time, I had lost a lot of respect for myself.)

But beneath all this, as under a graveyard pallor, or the noon-day sun, lay the fact that the leap demanded that I commit myself to the clear impossibility of becoming a writer, and attempting to save my family that way. I do not think I said this. I think Emile knew it.

I had hoped for a reprieve, hoped, on the marked Sunday, to get away, unnoticed: but I was the "young" Brother Baldwin, and I sat in the front row, and the pastor did not begin his sermon until about a quarter past one. Well. At one thirty, I—*tip-toed*—out. The further details of my departure do not concern us here: that was how I left the church.

I am fairly certain that the matinee, that Sunday, was *Native Son* (also directed by Orson Welles) at the St. James Theatre. We were in the balcony, and I remember standing up, abruptly and unwisely, when the play ended, and nearly falling headlong from the balcony to the pit. I did not know that I had been hit so hard: I will not forget Canada Lee's performance as long as I live.

Canada Lee was Bigger Thomas, but he was also Canada Lee: his physical presence, like the physical presence of Paul Robeson, gave me the right to live. He was not at the mercy of my imagination, as he would have been, on the screen: he was on the stage, in flesh and blood, and I was, therefore, at the mercy of *his* imagination.

For that long-ago *Macbeth* had both terrified and exhilarated me. I knew enough to know that the actress (the colored lady!) who played Lady Macbeth might very well be a janitor, or a janitor's wife, when the play closed, or when the curtain came down. Macbeth was a nigger, just like me, and I saw the witches in church, every Sunday, and all up and down the block, all week long, and Banquo's face was a familiar face. At the same time, the majesty and torment on that stage were real: indeed they revealed the play, *Macbeth*. They *were* those people and that torment was a torment I recognized, those were real daggers, it was real blood, and those crimes resounded and compounded, as real crimes do:

I did not have to ask, *what happens to them now?* And, if niggers have rhythm, these niggers had the beat—*tomorrow and tomorrow and tomorrow,* and—*thou shalt be King hereafter!* It is not accidental that I was carrying around the plot of a play in my head, and looking, with a new wonder (and a new terror) at everyone around me, when I suddenly found myself on the floor of the church, one Sunday, crying holy unto the Lord. Flesh and blood had proved to be too much for flesh and blood.

For, they were themselves, these actors—these people were themselves. They could *be* Macbeth only because they were themselves: my first real apprehension of the mortal challenge. Here, nothing corroborated any of my fantasies: flesh and blood was being challenged by flesh and blood. It is said that the camera cannot lie, but rarely do we allow it to do anything else, since the camera sees what you point it at: the camera sees what you want it to see. The language of the camera is the language of our dreams.

TWO

❦

Who Saw Him Die?
I, Said the Fly

If religion was a thing
money could buy,
The rich would live,
and the poor would die.

TRADITIONAL

I SHALL SPIT ON YOUR GRAVES is a French look at the black American problem. It is, also, an utterly cynical use of the name of Boris Vian, the young Frenchman who wrote the novel on which the film is emphatically *not* based. (I am told that Vian never saw the completed film. During the first screening of the film, he had a heart attack and died. The story may be apocryphal, but I can well believe it.)

Vian himself points out, somewhat savagely, that *I Shall Spit on Your Graves* is not a very good novel: he was enraged (and enlightened) by the vogue it had in France. This vogue was due partly to the fact that it was presented as Vian's translation of an American novel. But this vogue was due also to Vian himself, who was one of the most striking figures of a long-ago Saint-Germain des Prés. I am speaking of the immediate post-war years. Paris was then on bicycles: there were few cars, and gas (along with milk, cheese, and butter) was rationed. Juliette Greco was in the process of becoming famous in *Le Tabou*, and was often to be seen driving an ancient automobile: she was the envy of the neighborhood. Sydney Bechet and Claude Luter were playing together at *Le Vieux Colombier;* Kenny Clarke was soon to arrive. There were jam sessions over a theater in rue Fontaine which lasted until dawn, and sometimes until noon, at one of which jam sessions I first heard Annie Ross.

I was sitting at the Café Flore one afternoon when an enormous car, with baggage piled on the roof, stopped before the café. A large woman opened the car door, leaned out, and yelled, "Is Jean-Paul Sartre here today?" The waiter said, "No, madame," whereupon the car door slammed, and the car drove off. Camus's hour had yet so savagely to strike: and both men eventually disappeared from the Flore. The curious, and, on the whole, rather obvious doctrine of *l'existentialisme* flourished, and the word *négritude,* though it was beginning to be muttered, had yet to be heard. *I Shall Spit on Your Graves,* and Vian himself, and a tense, even rather terrified wonder about Americans, were part of this ferment: and, further, the straight-laced French (who had not yet heard of Jean Genêt, and who remain absolutely impervious to Rimbaud and Baudelaire) considered the novel pornographic.

One of the reasons—perhaps *the* reason—that the novel was considered pornographic is that it is concerned with the vindictive sexual aggression of one black man against many women. (At that moment in time, the black G.I. in Europe was a genuinely disturbing conundrum.) The novel takes place in America, and the black man looks like a white man—this double remove liberating both fantasy and hope, which is, perhaps, at bottom, what pornography is all about. This is certainly what that legend created by Rudolph Valentino, in *The Sheik,* is all about, as is made clear by his fan mail—poor boy!—and this fantasy and hope contain the root appeal of *Tarzan (King of The Apes!).* Both the Sheik and Tarzan are white men who look and act like black men—act like black men, that is, according to the white imagination which has created them: one can eat one's cake without having it, or one can have one's cake without eating it.

What informs Vian's book, however, is not sexual fantasy, but rage and pain: that rage and pain which Vian (almost alone) was able to hear in the black American musicians, in the bars, dives, and cellars, of the Paris of those years. In his book, a black man who can "cross the line" sets out to avenge the murder of his younger, darker brother; and the primary tool of this vengeance is—his tool. Vian would have known something of this from Faulkner, and from Richard Wright, and from Chester Himes, but he *heard* it in the music, and, indeed, he saw it in the streets. Vian's character is eventually uncovered, but not before he has seduced and murdered two of the richest and most attractive white women he can find. He is caught, and hanged—hung, like a horse, his sex, according to Vian, mocking his murders to the last. Vian did not know that this particular nigger would almost certainly have been castrated: which is but another and deadlier way for white men to be mocked by the terror and the fury by which they are engulfed upon the discovery that the black man is a man: "it hurt," says T. E. Lawrence, in *Seven Pillars of Wisdom,* "that they [the negroes]should possess exact counter-parts of all our bodies."

Vian's social details, as concerns American life, are all askew, but he had the sense to frame his story in such a way as to prevent these details from intruding. And he gets some things right, for example, the idle, self-centered, spoiled, erotic dreaming of a certain category of American youth: there are moments which bring to mind *Rebel Without a Cause*. For these children, the passage of time can mean only the acceleration of hostility and despair. In spite of the book's naïveté, Vian cared enough about his subject to force one into a confrontation with a certain kind of anguish. The book's power comes from the fact that he forces you to see this anguish from the undisguised viewpoint of his foreign, alienated own.

The film is quite another matter, having, for one thing, no viewpoint whatever except that from the window of the Stock Exchange. The film takes place, so we are endlessly informed, in Trenton: which is, in the film, a small, unbelievably unattractive town, just outside of Paris, on the road to New Orleans. In fact, it begins in (I guess) New Orleans, with a black boy, playing a harmonica, sitting on an immense bale of cotton which is being hoisted to the dock. The boy jumps off the bale of cotton, still playing his harmonica, starts walking; is grabbed around the neck by his affectionate, older, light white brother; and, alas, the film begins. The young black boy, who would appear to be about thirteen, seems to have been playing around with a white girl. (We do not, thank heaven, meet her.) His older brother warns him to be careful. Harmonica says that he will be. The brothers separate, and we next see and hear Harmonica in the cool of the evening (not yet in the heat of the night) unconcernedly walking along a deserted country road. Headlights flash behind him; white men leap out of their cars, the boy turns to face them; and the next time we see him, he is hanging from a tree.

His older light white brother cuts him down and carries him to where the darkies are assembled, beginning to moan—the darkies, that is. The older light white brother vows vengeance, over the Christian plea for forgiveness of the old black preacher, to whom he appears—though certainly not physically—to be related. He puts his brother's body on a table in the cabin, while the darkies watch; douses it with kerosene, while the darkies watch, and moan; lights a match, setting his brother, the cabin, and, presumably, the entire neighborhood aflame, while the darkies keep moaning; and, sensibly enough, leaves.

There follows a somewhat opaque episode, involving the French idea of a drunken, cowardly Southerner—an idea which is not absolutely inaccurate, bearing in mind that *New* Orleans is found in the state of *Louisiana,* for very precise reasons, and leaving aside the Haitian adventure, and to go, for the moment, no further than that—from whom our hero, indisputably *évolué,* needs credentials for Trenton: a city to be found, he has been told, in the North. For he is going North, he is going to "cross the line," and he is, in effect, black-mailing the Southern drunkard into being his accomplice. There is a great deal of unsuspenseful business with a loaded shotgun, but our hero gets the letter, throws the loaded shotgun toward the arms of his drunken friend, gets into his car, and drives off. (None of this paranoia is in Vian's book.) Our hero takes what is, in effect, his letter of racial credit to an aging bookstore owner in Trenton, and so we meet the far from merry maidens of our hero's grim desire.

Vian's book has a certain weary, mysogynistic humor—the chicks fuck like rabbits, or minks, and our hero gets a certain charge, or arrives at the mercy of a nearly unbearable ecstasy, out of his private knowledge that they are being fucked by a nigger:

he is committing the crime for which his brother was murdered, he is fucking these cunts with his brother's prick. And he comes three times, so to speak, each time he comes, once for his brother, and once for the "little death" of the orgasms to which he always brings the ladies, and, uncontrollably, for the real death to which he is determined to bring them. This intersection, where life disputes with death, is very vivid in the book: and it does not, of course, exist in the film.

In the book, one believes that the hero loved his brother, and to such a depth indeed that he is deliberately destroying his own sexuality—his hope of love—in order to keep faith with his destroyed brother: *the mortification of the flesh.* One may object that this is not exactly what Paul or Peter or The Bank of the Holy Ghost meant to say, but, incontestably, this is what has been accomplished: that the use of one's own body in the act of love is considered a crime against the Holy Ghost. No greater blasphemy against the human being can be imagined. One may remark that the hero's vengeance is not at all what the brother would have wanted, for his brother, but the younger brother is not there to speak for himself. The younger brother lives only in the memory of his older brother, and in the unanswerable light of an unforgivable crime.

This relentless need for something much deeper than revenge comes close to the truth of many lives, black and white: but revenge is not among the human possibilities. Revenge is a human dream. There is no way of conveying to the corpse the reasons you have made him one—you have the corpse, and you are, thereafter, at the mercy of a fact which missed the truth, which means that the corpse has you. On the other hand, the corpse doesn't want his murderer, either, and one is under the iron obligation not to allow oneself to be turned into one. The key is contained in the question of where the power lies—power, literally, and power on a more dreadful level—and Vian's anecdote pivots on the geometry of destruction and self-destruction. This is a delicate tightrope stretched taut and high, above unimaginable chasms, coming close to the truth of many black lives: many have fallen, but many have not. There is, indeed, far beyond and beneath the truth of Vian's anecdote, another truth, a truth which drags us into the icy and fiery center of a mystery: how have we endured? But the key word, there, is *we*.

In the film there is no brother, there are no brothers, there are no women, no passion, and no pain: there is the guilty, furtive, European notion of sex, a notion which obliterates any possibility of communion, or any hope of love. There is also the European dream of America—which, after all, is how we *got* America: a dream full of envy, guilt, condescension, and terror, a dream which began as an adventure in real estate. That song which Europe let out of its heart so long ago, to be sung on ships, and to cross all that water, is now coming back to Europe, perhaps to drive Europe mad: the return of the song will certainly render Europe obsolete, and return the North American wilderness—yet to be conquered!—to a truth which has nothing to do with Europe.

The Birth of a Nation is based on a novel I will almost certainly never read, *The Clansman*, by a certain Thomas Dixon, who achieved it sometime after the Civil War. He did not, oddly enough, write the 1952 film, *Storm Warning*, also about the Klan, starring Ginger Rogers, Steve Cochran, Ronald Reagan, and Doris Day. Unlike, and quite unjustly, *Storm Warning* (possibly because the Ginger Rogers film speaks courageously for the Union, and against the Confederacy), *The Birth of a Nation* is known as one of the great classics of the American cinema: and indeed it is.

It is impossible to do justice to the story, such story as attempts to make an appearance being immediately submerged by the tidal wave of the plot; and, in Griffith's handling of this fable, anyway, the key is to be found in the images. The film cannot be called dishonest: it has the Niagara force of an obsession.

A story is impelled by the necessity to reveal: the aim of the story is revelation, which means that a story can have nothing—at least not deliberately—to hide. This also means that a story resolves nothing. The resolution of a story must occur in us, with what we make of the questions with which the story leaves us. A plot, on the other hand, must come to a resolution, prove a point: a plot must answer all the questions which it pretends to pose. *In the Heat of the Night,* for example, turns on a plot, a plot designed to camouflage exceedingly bitter questions; it can be said, for *The Defiant Ones,* that it attempts to tell a story. The Book of Job is a story, the proof being that the details of Job's affliction never, for an instant, obscure Job from our view. This story has no resolution. We end where we began: everything Job has lost has been returned to him. And, yet, we are not quite where we began. We do not know what that voice out of the whirlwind will thunder next time—and we know that there will certainly be a next time. Job is not the same, nor are we: Job's story has changed Job forever, and illuminated us. By contrast, the elaborate anecdote of Joseph and his brothers turns on a plot, the key to which is that coat of many colors. That coat is meant to blind us to the fact that the anecdote of Joseph and his brothers, so far from being a record of brotherly love and forgiveness, is an absolutely deadly study of frustrated fratricide and frustrated (although elaborately disguised) revenge. When Joseph feeds his brothers, it is not an act of love: he could just as easily have let them starve, which they, very logically, expected him to do. They, just as logically, expected him to die when they threw him into the pit. Having done the unexpected once, Joseph can do it twice: *here is the brother who was thrown into a pit by you, my brothers, and left alone there to die!—help yourself, there's plenty.* Neither Joseph, nor, more importantly, perhaps, his brothers, have got past that day. It is an act which cannot be forgotten, any more than the branding iron on the skin can be forgotten. And, if it cannot be forgotten, which is to say undone, then it will certainly, in one way or another, be repeated: therefore, it cannot be forgiven: a grave matter, if one accepts my central premise, which is that all men are brothers.

Similarly, *The Birth of a Nation* is really an elaborate justification of mass murder. The film cannot possibly admit this, which is why we are immediately placed at the mercy of a plot labyrinthine and preposterous—as follows:

The gallant South, on the edge of the great betrayal by the Northern brethren: this is the pastoral and yet doom-laden weight of the early images. Two brothers, robust, two sisters, fair, a handsome house, a loving and united family, and happy, loyal slaves.

Unhappily, however, for the South, and for us all, a certain eminent Southern politician has a mulatto slave mistress—a house nigger, whose cot he shares when the sun goes down: she does not share his bed, to which he returns shortly before the sun comes up: and the baleful effect of this carnal creature on the eminent Southern politician helps bring about the ruin of the South. I cannot tell you exactly *how* she brings about so devastating a fate, and I defy anyone to tell *me:* but she does. Without attempting to track my way through any more of what we will call the pre-plot: the War comes. The South is shamefully defeated—or, not so much defeated, it would appear, as betrayed: by the influence of the mulattoes. For the previously noted eminent and now renegade Southern politician has also, as it turns out, a mulatto protégé (we do not know how this happened, but we are allowed to suspect the worst) and this mulatto protégé is maneuvered into the previously all-white Congress of the United States. At which point the Carpetbaggers arrive, and the movie begins. For the film is concerned with the Reconstruction, and how the birth of the Ku Klux Klan overcame that dismal and mistaken chapter in our—American—history.

The first image of the film is of the African slave's arrival. The image and the title both convey the European terror before the idea of the black and white, red and white, saved and pagan, confrontation. I think that it was Freud who suggested that the presence of the black man in America foreshadowed America's doom—which America, if it could not civilize these savages, would deserve: it is certainly the testimony of such disparate witnesses as William Faulkner and Isadora Duncan. For Marx and Engels, the presence of the black man in America was simply a useful crowbar for the liberation of whites: an idea which has had its issue in the history of American labor unions. The Founding Fathers shared this view, eminently, Thomas Jefferson, and The Great Emancipator freed those slaves he could not reach, in order to create, hopefully, a fifth column behind the Confederate lines. This ambivalence contains the key to American literature—all the way from *The Scarlet Letter* to *The Big Sleep.* In any case, what Europe really felt about the black presence in America is revealed by the stratagems the European-Americans have used, and use, to avoid it: that is, by American history, or the actual, present condition of any American city.

The first image, then, of *The Birth of a Nation* is immensely and unconsciously revealing. Were it not for their swarthy color—or not even that, so many immigrants having been transformed into white men only upon arrival, and, as it were, by decree—were it not for the title preceding the image: they would look exactly like European passengers, huddled, silent, patient, and hopeful, in the shadow of the Statue of Liberty. *(Give us your poor!* Many of the poor, not only in America, but all over the world, are beginning to find that these famous lines have a somewhat sinister ring.) These slaves look as though they *want* to enter the Promised Land, and are regarding their imminent masters in the hope of being bought.

This is not exactly the way blacks looked, of course, as they entered America, nor were they yet covered by European clothes. Blacks got here nearly as naked as the day they were born, and were sold that way, every inch of their anatomy exposed and examined, teeth to testicles, breast to bottom. That's how darkies were born: more to the point, here, it is certainly how mulattoes were born.

For, the most striking thing about the merciless plot on which *The Birth of a Nation* depends is that, although the legend of the nigger controls it the way the day may be controlled by threat of rain, there are really no niggers in it. The plot is entirely controlled by the image of the mulatto, and there are two of them, one male and one female. All of the energy of the film is siphoned off into these two dreadful and improbable creatures. It might have made sense—that is, might have made a story—if these two mulattoes had been related to each other, or to the renegade politician, whose wards they are: but, no, he seems to have dreamed them up (they *are* like creatures in a nightmare *someone* is having) and they are related to each other only by their envy of white people. The renegade politician, I should already have told you—but this is one of the difficulties of trying to follow a plot—is also the heroine's father. This fact brings about his belated enlightenment, the final victory of the Klan, the film's denouement, and a double wedding.

I am leaving a great deal out, but, in any case, the renegade politician is brought brutally to his senses when his mulatto ward, now a rising congressman, so far forgets himself as to offer himself in marriage to the renegade politician's beautiful daughter, Miss Lillian Gish. The Klan rides out in fury, making short work of the ruffian, and others like him. The niggers are last seen, heads averted and eyes down, returning to their cabins—none of which have been burned, apparently, there being no point in burning empty cabins—and the South rises triumphantly to its feet.

It is not clear what happens to the one presumably remaining mulatto, the female. Neither of the two mulattoes had any sexual interest in the other; given what we see of their charms, this is quite understandable. Both are driven by a hideous lust for whites, she for the master, he for the maid: they are, at least, thank heaven, heterosexual, due, probably, to their lack of imagination.

Their lust for the whites, however, is of such a nature that it suffers from all the manifestations of hysterical hatred. And this is not quite so understandable, except in the gaudy light of the film's intention. The film presents us, after all, with the spectacle of a noble planet, brought to such a pass that even their loyal slaves are subverted. For the sake of the dignity of this temporarily defeated people, and out of a vivid and loving concern for their betrayed and endangered slaves, the violated social order must, at all costs, be re-established. And it *is* re-established by the vision and heroism of the noblest (and, in future, overt), has been brought about, not through any fault of their own, and not because of any defection among their slaves, but by the weak and misguided among them who have given the mulattoes ideas above their station.

But how did so ungodly a creature as the mulatto enter this Eden, and where did he come from?

The film cannot concern itself with this inconvenient and impertinent question, any more than can Governor Wallace, or the bulk of his confreres, North or South. We need not pursue it, except to observe that almost all mulattoes, and especially at that time, were produced by white men, and rarely indeed by an act of love. The mildest possible word is coercion: which is why white men invented the crime of rape, with the specific intention (and effect) of castrating and hanging the nigger. Neither did black men fasten on the word, *mulatto,* to describe the issue of their loins. But white men did—as follows:

The root of the word, *mulatto,* is Spanish, according to Webster, from *mulo,* a mule. The word refers to: (1) a person, one of whose parents is Negro and the other Caucasian, or white; and (2) popularly, any person with mixed Negro and Caucasian ancestry.

A mule is defined as (1) the offspring of a donkey and a horse, especially the offspring of a jackass and a mare—*mules are usually sterile*. And, a further definition: in biology, a hybrid, *especially a sterile hybrid*. (Italics mine.)

The idea of producing a child, on condition, and under the guarantee, that the child cannot reproduce must, after all, be relatively rare: no matter how dim a view one may take of the human race. It argues an extraordinary spiritual condition, or an unspeakable spiritual poverty: to produce a child with the intention of using it to gain a lease on limbo, or, failing that, on purgatory: to produce a child with the extinction of the child as one's hope of heaven. *Mulatto:* for that outpost of Christianity, that segment of the race which called itself white, which found itself stranded among the heathen on the North American continent, under the necessity of destroying all evidence of sin, including, if need be, those children who were proof of abandonment to savage, heathen passion, and under the absolute necessity of preserving its idea of itself by any means necessary, the use of the word, *mulatto*, was by no means inadvertent. It was one of the keys to American history, present, and past. Americans are still destroying their own children: and, infanticide being but a step away from genocide, not only theirs. If we do not know where the mulatto came from, we certainly know where a multitude went, dispatched by their own fathers, and we know where multitudes are, until today, plotting death, plotting life, groaning in the chains in which their fathers have bound them.

Our fathers, indeed, for here we all are: and we encounter an invitation to discover the essential decency of this history (this is known as progress) in the person of the Sheriff in a film made some fifty-odd years later, *In the Heat of the Night*.

This film has no mulattoes: unless one wishes to examine,

with a certain rigor, the roles played by some of the townspeople: we will return to this speculation: and, apart from the brief cotton-picking sequence, seen from the window of the Sheriff's moving car, it is hard to locate the niggers. (This, also, is progress.) The man who lodges the black detective comes close to being a nigger. The lady who arranges abortions is dark indeed, but is clearly passing—through; and Mr. Virgil Tibbs comes from freedom-loving Philadelphia, the city of brotherly love. To this haven, he will return, if he lives. But we know that he *will* live. The star of a film is rarely put to death, and certainly not *this* star, and certainly not in this film.

The entire burden, therefore, of such suspense as the film may claim to have falls squarely on the shoulders of the Sheriff (Rod Steiger). The life of Virgil Tibbs (Sidney Poitier) is endangered precisely to the extent that we are concerned about the salvation of the Sheriff's soul. One ought, indeed, I suppose, to be concerned about the soul of any descendant of *The Birth of a Nation,* and the Sheriff is certainly such a descendant, as is the film itself. On the other hand, it is difficult to sustain such a concern when the concern is not reciprocal, and if this concern demands one's complicity in a lie: which state of affairs, having gone beyond progress, is sometimes called brotherhood, the achievement of which state of grace is exactly what *In the Heat of the Night* imagines itself to be about.

The film is breathtaking, not to say vertiginous, in the speed with which it moves from one preposterous proposition to another. We are asked to believe that a grown black man, who knows the South, and who, being a policeman, must know something about his colleagues, both South and North, would elect to change trains in a Southern backwater at that hour of the early morning and sit alone in the waiting room; that the Sheriff imagines that he needs a confession from this black Northern vagrant, and so elects to converse with him before locking him up, turning him over to his deputies, and closing the case. (Of course, it is suggested, at that moment—and quite helplessly, the truth of the white and black male meeting living far beneath the moment of this manipulated scene—that the Sheriff is being something of a sadist, and is playing cat and mouse.) And the film betrays itself, in the early sequences, in quite a curious way. One might suppose, after all, since the film was made *after* the 1964 Civil Rights Act, that the Sheriff might be concerned about the pressure which might be brought to bear by the Federal Government: but this possibility, astoundingly enough, does not appear to enter his mind. He reacts to the fact that the black man makes more money than he does which has the effect of eliciting our sympathy for this doubly poor white man. Virgil's continued presence on the case is due entirely to the reaction of the widow of the murdered man; this man, conveniently enough (as concerns the necessities of the plot) was in the process of bringing new industry to the town when he was murdered. As the man's widow, she now has the power to transfer this potential wealth to another town, which she will do if Virgil is not allowed to continue his investigation of her husband's murder. This convolution of the plot really demands a separate essay: it contains so many oblique and unconscious confessions concerning the roles of money, sex, marriage, greed, and guilt and power. In any case, the widow, having done her bit, disappears, and the town is stuck with Virgil. So is the Sheriff: and the Sheriff just don't know, now, if he glad or if he bad: but he got to do his best to look bad.

What kind of people are you? the widow cries out at one point in the film: as well she might. There is something really stunning—cunning is too loaded a word—in the casting of this film. Poitier's presence gives the film its only real virility, and so emphatically indeed that the emotional climate of the film is that of a mysteriously choked and baffled—and yet compulsive—act of contrition. This virility is not in the least compromised by the fact that he has no woman, visibly: on the contrary, it is thus reinforced, since we know that he is saving himself for Philadelphia, where *they call me Mr. Tibbs!* The wealth of his health is presented in very powerful contrast to the poverty and infirmity of the white men by whom he is surrounded, and is the only genuinely positive element the film contains. It coats the film lightly, so to speak, with a kind of desperately boyish, unadmitted anguish. But that the film cannot or dare not pursue the implications of this sorrow is made very clear in that choked and opaque scene between the black detective and the Sheriff, in the latter's living room, over bourbon. The chief deputy, Sam (Warren Oates), in terms of the weights and balances of the film has the best assignment, his role allowing him to be absolutely truthful, though never deep. Sam drives his patrol car, each night, off his route to watch a naked girl through the windows of her house. She is to be found thus, apparently, every night, at the hour that Sam drives by: and, so far as the film informs us, this is their only connection—a rather horrifying thought, when one considers how much of the truth it contains, for lives like that, and in such a town.

The girl is a poor white, and is as marked by this misfortune as are the mulattoes of *The Birth of a Nation*, and she has a poor white brother, who appears to know nothing at all about his sister. There is the white boy, picked up for the murder after Virgil

Tibbs's credentials have been established, and Virgil has agreed to remain on the case, or been coerced into doing so: this boy first hates, then learns to love the black cop who clears him, and saves his life. And there is the waiter in the diner, who refuses to serve Virgil Tibbs. This is an utterly grotesque creature, as hysterical as *Nation's* mulatto maid, presented as being virtually biologically inferior to everyone else. He, it turns out, is the lover of the ex-hibitionistic girl—a circumstance which one does not believe for a moment, not even in that sleepy little town—and he is the father of the child she is expecting. He is, also, the murderer. He committed the murder because (I think) he needed money for an abortion. The climactic scene, anyway, takes place outside the establishment of the lady who deals in abortions. This is an exciting scene indeed, but before I try to deal with this excitement, there are a couple of other scenes we should consider.

One is the scene in the hothouse of the wealthy horticulturist, who is presented as being one of the most powerful men of the region. In this scene, Tibbs exhibits a somewhat unexpected knowledge of varieties of plant life. This allows his host to make clear his racial bias. ("These plants are delicate. They like the nigras. They need care.") One thing leads to another, so to speak, and, eventually, the wealthy horticulturist slaps Tibbs in the face. Under the eyes of the Sheriff, Tibbs slaps him back. The wealthy host is astonished that the Sheriff does not shoot Tibbs on the spot: the Sheriff, furious that anyone should suppose him capable of so base an action, throws his chewing gum on the ground (of the powerful host) and stalks out, after Virgil. The wealthy landowner ("There was a day when I could have had you shot!") looks on in disbelief, and we leave him weeping, possibly because his day has passed. End of joke.

Then, there is the scene with the lady who deals in abortions. I have described this lady somewhat rudely; she may have passed through the West Indies, or Africa, and, at that, speedily; but she surely do not come from around here. She appears to be looking for a home, and, from the way Virgil Tibbs treats her, no wonder—I would, too. Demanding to know who, in the town, is paying for an abortion, he informs her (speaking of the prison sentence with which he is threatening her) that "there's white time and black time—and ain't nothing worse than black time!" The lady who deals in abortions appears to be utterly astounded and downcast by this news and rolls her eyes toward (I suppose) her suitcase. But she is saved by the arrival of the exhibitionistic girl: who, seeing Virgil Tibbs (they have met before), runs out into the night.

Virgil runs after her (while the lady who deals in abortions flees into the back room, to pack, and book passage to Canada, or Algeria) and picks up the fleeing poor white chick in his arms. In this unlucky posture he is found as headlights flash, before, and behind, and all around him, and white men leap out of their cars: into the heat of the night.

This is the penultimate, exciting scene. One of the white men is the poor white brother of the poor white girl, and, naturally, he intends to lynch the nigger, whose black hands are still on the body of his white sister. With great presence of mind, Mr. Tibbs drops the sister and points to the real killer, who has the money for the abortion in his pocket. The attention of the murderous mob is thus distracted, naturally, from the nigger and the white chick to this creep, who promptly shoots the brother, dead: end of exciting scene.

There remains the obligatory, fade-out kiss. I am aware that men do not kiss each other in American films, nor, for the most part, in America, nor do the black detective and the white Sheriff kiss here. But the obligatory, fade-out kiss, in the classic American film, did not really speak of love, and, still less, of sex: it spoke of reconciliation, of all things now becoming possible. It was a device desperately needed among a people for whom so much had to be made possible. And, no matter how inept one must judge this film to be, in spite of its absolutely appalling distance from reality, in spite of my own helplessly sardonic tone when discussing it, and even in spite of the fact that the effect of such a film is to increase and not lessen white confusion and complacency, and black rage and despair, I still do not wish to be guilty of the gratuitous injustice of seeming to impute base motives to the people responsible for its existence. Our situation would be far more coherent if it were possible to categorize, or dismiss, *In the Heat of the Night* so painlessly. No: the film helplessly conveys—without confronting—the anguish of people trapped in a legend. They cannot live within this legend; neither can they step out of it. The film gave me the impression, according to my notes the day I saw it, of "something strangling, alive, struggling to get out." And I certainly felt this during the final scene, when the white Sheriff takes the black detective's bag as they walk to the train. It is not that the creators of the film were inspired by base motives, but that they could not understand their motives, nor be responsible for the effect of their exceedingly complex motives, in action. (All motives are complex, and it is just as well to remember this: including, or perhaps especially, one's own.) The history which produces such a film cannot, after all, be swiftly understood, nor can the effects of this history be easily resolved. Nor can this history be blamed on any single individual; but, at the same time, no one can be let off the hook. It is a terrible thing, simply, to be trapped in one's history, and attempt, in the same motion (and in this, our life!) to accept, deny, reject, and redeem it—and, also, on whatever level, to profit from it. And: with one's head in the fetid jaws of this lion's mouth, attempt to love and be loved, and raise one's children, and pay the rent, and wrestle with one's mortality. In the final scene at the station, there is something choked and moving, something sensed through a thick glass, dimly, in the Sheriff's sweet, boyish, Southern injunction, to Virgil, "take care, you hear?" and something equally choked and rigid in the black detective's reaction. It reminded me of nothing so much as William Blake's *Little Black Boy*—that remote, that romantic, and that hopeless. Virgil Tibbs goes to where they call him *Mister,* far away, presumably, from South Street, and the Sheriff has gone back to the niggers, who are really his only assignment. And nothing, alas, has been made possible by this obligatory, fade-out kiss, this preposterous adventure: except that white Americans have been encouraged to continue dreaming, and black Americans have been alerted to the necessity of waking up. People who cannot escape thinking of themselves as white are poorly equipped, if equipped at all, to consider the meaning of black: people who know so little about themselves can face very little in another: and one dare hope for nothing from friends like these. This cruel observation is implicit in the script: for what would have happened to our Mr. Tibbs, or, indeed, to our Sheriff, had the widow demanded the black man's blood as the price for the wealth she was bringing into the town? Who, among that manly crew, would have resisted the widow's might? The people of *In the Heat of the Night* can be considered moving and pathetic only if one has the luxury of the assurance that one will never be at their mercy. And that no one in the world has the luxury of this assurance is beginning to be clear: all over the world.

In *The Birth of a Nation,* the Sheriff would have been an officer of the Klan. The widow would, secretly, have been sewing Klan insignia. The murdered man (whether or not he was her husband) would have been a carpetbagger. Sam would have been a Klan deputy. The troublesome poor whites would have been mulattoes. And Virgil Tibbs would have been the hunted, not the hunter. It is impossible to pretend that this state of affairs has really altered: a black man, in any case, had certainly best not believe everything he sees in the movies.

In 1942, Bette Davis, under the direction of John Huston, delivered a ruthlessly accurate (and much underrated) portrait of a Southern girl, in the Warner Brothers production of Ellen Glasgow's novel, *In This, Our Life.* She thus became, and, indeed, remained, the toast of Harlem because her prison scene with the black chauffeur was cut when the movie came uptown. The uproar in Harlem was impressive, and I think that the scene was reinserted; in any case, either uptown or downtown, I saw it. Davis appeared to have read, and grasped, the script—which must have made her rather lonely—and she certainly understood the role. Her performance had the effect, rather, of exposing and shattering the film, so that she played in a kind of vacuum: much the same thing was to happen, later, to Sidney Poitier, with his creation of Noah Cullen, in *The Defiant Ones.*

In *In This, Our Life,* Davis is a spoiled Southern girl, guilty of murder in a hit-and-run automobile accident, and she has blamed this crime on her black chauffeur. (An actor named Ernest Anderson: Hattie McDaniel played his mother.) But he has steadfastly denied having had the car that night. She, armed with her wealth, her color, and her sex, goes to the prison to persuade him to corroborate her story: and what she uses, through jail-house bars, is her sex. She will pay, for the chauffeur's silence, any price he demands. Indeed, the price is implicit in the fact that she knows he knows that she is guilty: she can have no secrets from him now.

Blacks are often confronted, in American life, with such devastating examples of the white descent from dignity; devastating not only because of the enormity of the white pretensions, but because this swift and graceless descent would seem to indicate that white people have no principles whatever. At the beginning of the Attica uprising, for example, a white guard was heard pleading with a black prisoner: "You can have anything you want," the guard is reported to have said. "You can have *me*. Just don't send me out there."

In the film, the black chauffeur simply does not trust the white girl to keep her end of the bargain—which would involve using her power to save his life—and is far too proud, anyway, to strike such a bargain. But the offer has been made, and the truth about the woman revealed.

The blacks have a song which says, *I can't believe what you say, because I see what you do.* No American film, relating to blacks, can possibly incorporate this observation. This observation—set to music, as are so many black observations—denies, simply, the validity of the legend which is responsible for these films; films which exist for the sole purpose of perpetuating the legend.

Black men, after all, have been the lovers, and victims, of women like the woman in *In This, Our Life:* and these women have also been the victims of black men: and sometimes they have loved each other; and sometimes had to live in hell to pay for it. Even the most thoughtless, even the most deluded black person knows more about his life than the image he is offered as the justification of it. Black men know something about white sheriffs. They know, for one thing, that the sheriff is no freer to become friends with them than they are to become friends with the sheriff: For example:

A white taxi driver once drove me from the airport in Birmingham, Alabama, to the Gaston Motel. This is a long, dark, tree-lined drive, and the taxi driver was breaking the law: for a white taxi driver is not—or was not, it is hard to be accurate concerning the pace of my country's progress—allowed to pick up a black fare. That this was not a wicked man is proven, perhaps, by the fact that I am still here. But I was in his cab only because the idea of waiting another hour at the airport (sitting on my typewriter, which I never carried South again) was too frightening. I had had no choice but to gamble on him. Yet, I could not be at ease about his motives in breaking the law for a black, Northern journalist. It was perfectly possible, after all, that he had no intention of driving me to the Gaston Motel (which had already been bombed three times) but to my death. And there was no way for this thought not to have entered my mind: I would have had to be mindless not to have thought it. And what was he thinking? For, I felt that he wanted to talk to me, and I certainly wanted to talk to him. But neither of us could manage it. It was not his fault, and it was not my fault. We could find no way out of our common trouble, for we had been forbidden—and on pain of death—to trust, or to use, our common humanity, that confrontation and acceptance which is all that can save another human being.

Blacks know something about black cops, too, even those called Mister, in Philadelphia. They know that their presence on the force doesn't change the force or the judges or the lawyers or the bondsmen or the jails. They know the black cop's mother and his father, they may have met the sister, and they know the younger, or the older brother, who may be a bondsman, or a junkie, or a student, in limbo, at Yale. They know how much the black cop has to prove, and how limited are his means of proving it: where I grew up, black cops were yet more terrifying than white ones.

I think that it was T. S. Eliot who observed that the people cannot bear very much reality. This may be true enough, as far as it goes, so much depending on what the word "people" brings to mind: I think that we bear a little more reality than we might wish. In any case, in order for a person to bear his life, he needs a valid re-creation of that life, which is why, as Ray Charles might put it, blacks chose to sing the blues. This is why *Raisin in the Sun* meant so much to black people—on the stage: the film is another matter. In the theater, a current flowed back and forth between the audience and the actors: flesh and blood corroborating flesh and blood—as we say, testifying. The filmed play, which is all, alas, that *Raisin* is on film, simply stayed up there, on that screen. The unimaginative rigidity of the film locked the audience out of it. Furthermore, the people in *Raisin* are not the people one goes to the movies to see. The root argument of the play is really far more subtle than either its detractors or the bulk of its admirers were able to see.

The Defiant Ones, on the other hand, *is* a film, with people we are accustomed to seeing in the movies. Well: all except one. The irreducible difficulty of this genuinely well-meaning film is that no one, clearly, was able to foresee what Poitier would do with his role—nor was anyone, thereafter, able to undo it—and his performance, which lends the film its only real distinction, also, paradoxically, smashes it to pieces. There is no way to believe both Noah Cullen *and* the story. With the best will in the world, it is virtually impossible to watch Tony Curtis while Sidney is on the screen, or, with the possible exception of Lon Chaney, Jr., anyone else. It is impossible to accept the premise of the story, a premise based on the profound American misunderstanding of the nature of the hatred between black and white. There is a hatred—certainly: though I am now using this word with great caution, and only in the light of the effects, or the results, of hatred. But the hatred is not equal on both sides, for it does not have the same roots. This is, perhaps, a very subtle argument, but black men do not have the same reason to hate white men as white men have to hate blacks. The root of the white man's hatred is terror, a bottomless and nameless terror, which focuses on the black, surfacing, and concentrating on this dread figure, an entity which lives only in his mind. But the root of the black man's hatred is rage, and he does not so much hate white men as simply want them out of his way, and, more than that, out of his children's way. When the white man begins to have in the black man's mind the weight that the black man has in the white man's mind, that black man is going mad. And when he goes under, he does not go under screaming in terror: he goes under howling with rage. A black man knows that two men chained together have to learn to forage, eat, fart, shit, piss, and tremble, and sleep together: they are indispensable to each other, and anything can happen between them, and anyone who has been there knows this. No black man, in such a situation, and especially knowing what Poitier conveys so vividly Noah Cullen knows, would rise to the bait proffered by this dimwitted poor white child, whose only real complaint is that he is a bona-fide mediocrity who failed to make it in the American rat-race. But many, no better than he, and many much worse, make it every day, all the way to Washington: sometimes, indeed, via Hollywood. It is a species of cowardice, grave indeed, to pretend that black men do not know this. And it is a matter of the most disastrous sentimentality to attempt to bring black men into the white American nightmare, and on the same terms, moreover, which make life for white men all but intolerable.

It is this which black audiences resented about *The Defiant Ones:* that Sidney was in company far beneath him, and that the unmistakable truth of his performance was being placed at the mercy of a lie. Liberal white audiences applauded when Sidney, at the end of the film, jumped off the train in order not to abandon his white buddy. The Harlem audience was outraged, and yelled, *Get back on the train, you fool!* And yet, even at that, recognized, in Sidney's face, at the very end, as he sings "Sewing Machine," something noble, true, and terrible, something out of which we come: I have heard exasperated black voices mutter, more than once, *Lord, have mercy on these children, have* mercy—! *they just don't* know.

There is an image in *The Defiant Ones* which suggests the truth it can neither face nor articulate; and there is a sequence which gives the film completely away. The image occurs when the little boy has been disarmed, and, accidentally, knocked unconscious. The two fugitives are anxiously trying to revive him.

When the boy comes to, he looks up and sees Sidney's black face over him: and we see this face from the boy's point of view, and as the boy sees it: black, unreadable, not quite in focus—and, with a moving, and, as I take it, deliberate irony, this image is the single most beautiful image in the film. The boy screams in terror, and turns to the white man for protection; and the white man assures him that he needs no protection from the black man he was cursing when the boy came along.

We are trembling on the edge of confession here, for, of course, the way the little boy sees the black face is exactly the way the man sees it. It is a presence vaguely, but mightily threatening, partly because of its strangeness and privacy, but also because of its beauty: that beauty which lives so tormentedly in the eye of the white beholder. The film cannot pursue this perception, or suspicion, without bringing into focus the question of white maturity, or white masculinity. This is not the ostensible subject of *The Defiant Ones*. Yet, the dilemma with which we are confronted in the film can only begin to be unlocked on that level, precisely, which the film is compelled to avoid.

In the next sequence, they go along to the home of the boy's mother, who lives alone with her child. The husband, or the father, has been long gone. This sequence is crucial, containing the only justification for the ending of the film, and it deserves a little scrutiny.

The woman who now enters the picture has already been abandoned; and, in quite another sense, once she sees the white boy, is anxious to *be* abandoned. She has the tools which allow the two men to destroy the manacles and break the chain which has bound them together for so long.

The logic of actuality would now strongly indicate, given their situation, and what we have seen of their relationship, that they separate. For one thing, each fugitive is safer without the other, and, for another, the woman clearly wishes to be alone with the white boy. She feeds them both, first asking the white boy if he wants her to feed the black one. He says that he does, and they eat. It is unlikely that Noah Cullen would have sat still for this scene, and even more unlikely that he would obligingly fall asleep at the table while the white boy and the woman make love.

Of course, what the film is now attempting to say—consciously—is that the ordeal of the black man and the white man has brought them closer together than they ever imagined they could be. The fact, and the effect, of this particular ordeal is being offered as a metaphor for the ordeal of black-white relations in America, an ordeal, the film is saying, which has brought us closer together than we know. But the only level on which this can be said to be true is that level of human experience—that depth—of which Americans are most terrified. The complex of conflicting terrors which the black-white connection engenders is suggested by the turgidity of the action which ends this film.

For, when the morning comes, the white boy has elected to throw in his lot with the woman, which means that Noah, after all, is to brave the swamps, and ride the rails, alone.

Noah accepts this, with a briefly mocking bitterness, and he goes. The white boy and the woman begin preparing for their journey. The white boy is worried about his black buddy; though it is difficult to guess at what point, precisely, he begins to think of Noah as his buddy; and wonders, aloud, if he'll be all right. Whereupon, the woman tells him that she has deliberately given Noah instructions which will lead him to his death: that he will never get out of the swamps alive.

It is absolutely impossible to locate the woman's motive for conveying this information. Once Noah has walked out of her door, he is long gone, simply, and can pose no threat. It cannot conceivably matter to her whether he lives, or dies: he has left their lives, in any case, never to return. If she, for whatever reason, has found a means to make certain that he dies, it is impossible to believe that she would risk telling her newfound lover this. She does not know enough about him. The woman is presented as a kind of pathetic, unthinking racist. But she cannot be so unthinking (no woman is) as to take for granted that the man she met last night will approve of being made, in fact, her accomplice in murder. After all, she knows only that the man she met last night ordered her to feed the black boy: and the white boy who orders you to feed his black boy may not be willing to authorize you to kill him. This is not only *what every woman knows*, it is, more crucially, what every white Southern woman knows.

It would appear, however, that this revelation on the part of the woman has the effect of opening our white hero's eyes to the bottomless evil of racial hatred, and, after a stormy scene—a scene quite remarkably unconvincing—and, after the little boy has shot him in the shoulder, our hero lights out for the swamps, and Noah. He finds Noah, and they head for the train—Lord, that Hollywood train, forever coming round the bend!—but the gunshot wound slows the white boy up. Noah refuses to leave him—*you're dragging on the chain!* he cries, stretching out his arm. They get to the train, the black man jumps on, but the white boy can't make it, and the black man jumps off the train, it is hard, indeed, to say why.

Well. He jumps off the train in order to reassure white people, to make them know that they are not hated; that, though they have made human errors, they have done nothing for which to be hated. Well, blacks may or may not hate whites, and when they do, as I have tried to indicate, it's in their fashion. Whites may or may not deserve to be hated, depending on how one manipulates one's reserves of energy, and what one makes of history: in any case, the reassurance is false, the need ignoble, and the question, in this context, absolutely irrelevant. The question operates to hide the question: for what has actually happened, at the end of *The Defiant Ones,* is that a white male and a white female have come together, but are menaced by the presence of the black man. The white woman, therefore, eliminates the black man, so that she and the white man can be alone together. But the white man cannot endure this rupture—from what one must, here, perhaps, call his other, better, worse, or deeper self—and so rejects the white woman, crashing through the swamps, and braving death, in order to regain his black buddy. And his black buddy is waiting for him, and, eventually, takes him in his arms. The white boy has given up his woman. The black man has given up his hope of freedom: and what are we to make of such rigorous choices, so rigorously arrived at?

The choices do not involve, for example, that seismographic shudder which the word, *homosexual,* until today, produces in the American mind, or soul: I doubt that Americans will ever be able to face the fact that the word, homosexual, is not a noun. The root of this word, as Americans use it—or, as this word uses Americans—simply involves a terror of any human touch, since any human touch can change you. A black man and a white man can come together only in the absence of women: which is, simply, the American legend of masculinity brought to its highest pressure, and revealed, as it were, in black and white.

In black and white: the late James Edwards, and Lloyd Bridges, in the long-ago *Home of the Brave,* love each other, as friends must, and as men do. But the fact that one is black and one is white eliminates the possibility of the female presence, according, that is, to the American theology: *may the best man win!* In the black-white context, this elicits, simply, white paranoia: it is hard to imagine anything more abjectly infantile, or anything more tragic.

The film takes place in the heat of the jungles of the Second World War. The white boy loses his life immediately after a quarrel with the black boy. The quarrel is intense. The black boy imagines—hears, though the word is not spoken—that the white boy, his buddy, is about to call him nigger, or an approximation thereof. The nature of the military crisis forces them, at that precise moment, to separate: the white boy does not join them on the beach, where the boats are waiting to rescue our people from the Japanese. The black boy crawls back through the jungle, to find his dying friend, who dies in his arms. Then, guilt paralyzes him, physically, and he undergoes psychotherapy (the central action of the film) and, cured, able to walk, walks into the sunset with another victim, a white, one-armed veteran, to start a business—one dare not say a life—together. The doomed connect, again without women: *Coward,* says the one-armed white victim to that definitive victim, the black, *take my coward's hand.*

Okay. But why is the price of what should, after all, be a simple human connection so high? Is it really necessary to lose a woman, an arm, or one's mind, in order to say hello? And, let's face it, kids, men suffer from penis envy on quite another level than women do, a crucial matter if yours is black and mine is white: furthermore, no matter what Saint Paul may thunder, love is where you find it. A man can fall in love with a man: incarceration, torture, fire, and death, and, still more, the threat of these, have not been able to prevent it, and never will. It became a grave, a tragic matter, on the North American continent, where white power became indistinguishable from the question of sexual dominance. But the question of sexual dominance can exist only in the nightmare of that soul which has armed itself, totally, against the possibility of the changing motion of conquest and surrender, which is love.

The immense quantity of polish expended on *Guess Who's Coming to Dinner* is meant to blind one to its essential inertia and despair. A black person can make nothing of this film—except, perhaps, *Superfly*—and, when one tries to guess what white people make of it, a certain chill goes down the spine. A thirty-seven-year-old black doctor, for whom the word "prodigy" is simply ridiculously inadequate, has met a white girl somewhere in his travels, and they have come, together, to the home of the girl's parents, in San Francisco, to announce their intention to marry each other. Since the girl does not doubt, and has no reason to doubt, her parents' approval, this trip would not seem to be necessary. However, she may wish, merely, to exhibit her remarkable catch to San Francisco: or, to put it in less speculative terms, we are, again, at the mercy of a plot. The wonder doctor is Sidney Poitier, and the girl's parents are Spencer Tracy and Katharine Hepburn: which means that the question of parental blessing is immediately robbed of the remotest suspense: these winning, intelligent, and forward-looking people can certainly not object. The girl's mother, after an initial shock, is won over, almost at once. The father is dubious, cranky, and crotchety, but we know that his heart is in the right place—otherwise, Spencer Tracy would never have been cast in the part. The wonder doctor's parents (significantly) do not really pose a problem, and they enter the picture late—we will speak of them later.

The suspense, then, concerning this interracial marriage, can be created only by the black doctor. We gather that he has been married before, to a black woman, who died. This informs us that, in spite of his brilliance, he is not presumptuous, and he is not an upstart, unstable adventurer: nothing less than real love would have driven him so far beyond the boundaries of caste. This love is, also, quite remarkably self-effacing. He informs the girl's parents that, even though their daughter may be prepared to marry *him* without their consent, *he* will not marry *her* without it. The girl loves her parents too much, he explains, to be able to endure such a rupture; nor can he himself, for reasons of his own, bear to be the author of such pain.

Since history affords so few examples of this species of restraint on the part of the prospective bridegroom, perhaps we should take a closer look at him: and try to find out what he is actually saying. I scarcely have the heart to indicate the echoes to be found, here, of *In Abraham's Bosom* (yes: the supplicant of Paul Green's *In Abraham's Bosom)* nor do more than indicate the existence of Eugene O'Neill's *All God's Chillun Got Wings,* or the terror underlying *The Hairy Ape:* not now can I tell you: the road was rocky. The setting of *Guess Who's Coming to Dinner* is the key. We are on the heights of San Francisco—at a time not too far removed from the moment when the city of San Francisco reclaimed the land at Hunter's Point and urban-renewalized the niggers out of it. The difficult and terrified city, where the niggers are, lives far beneath these heights. The father is in a perfectly respectable, perhaps even admirable profession, and the mother runs an art gallery. The setting is a brilliant re-creation of a certain—and far from unattractive—level of American life. And the black doctor is saying, among other things, that his presence in this landscape (this hard-won Eden) will do nothing to threaten, or defile it—indeed, since in the event that he marries the girl, they are immediately going to the Far East, or some such place, he will not even be present. One can scarcely imagine striking a bargain more painless; and without even losing a daughter, who will, merely, in effect, be traveling, and broadening her education; keeping in touch via trans-Pacific telephone, and coming home to San Francisco from time to time, with her yet more various, toddling, and exotic acquisitions.

This moment in the film is handled with such skill that one would certainly prefer to believe it, if one could. Only the fact that one does not believe it prevents one from resenting it. No man in love is so easily prepared to surrender his beloved, or travel so many thousands of miles to do so: no one expects such behavior from Steve McQueen. Without belaboring this sufficiently glaring point, the basis for such suspense as the film may hope to claim having now been established, we are confronted with a series of classical tableaux:

We have already met the white, backward, uneducated taxi driver, mightily displeased by the glimpse he catches, in his rear-view mirror, of our lovers, kissing. He conveys his displeasure, failing to shake the doctor's cool: indeed, the doctor tips him.

We have already met the mother's assistant at the art gallery, a white woman, along with a particularly gruesome (and very cunningly used) example of modern art. The doctor toys with this dreadful object, as he toys with the woman's avid curiosity, and our lovers leave.

We meet the mother and the father, distressed domestic tête-à-tête, etc.—at which point we are informed of the doctor's staggering achievements—and now we meet the loyal nigger maid.

It so happened that I saw *The Birth of a Nation* and *Guess*

Who's Coming to Dinner on the same day—the first in the morning, the second in the afternoon. It happened, also, that I saw both films in the company of a young African girl, a Cameroons journalist. This girl has never seen America, and, understandably, took my testimony concerning my country with enormous grains of salt.

Yet, it was not my testimony which presented us, on the same day, in two films divided from each other by something like half a century, with the same loyal nigger maid, playing the same role, and speaking the same lines. In *The Birth of a Nation,* the loyal nigger maid informs the nigger congressman that she don't like niggers who set themselves up above their station. When our black wonder doctor hits San Francisco, some fifty-odd years later, he encounters exactly the same maid, who tells him exactly the same thing, for the same reason, and in the same words, adding, merely, as a concession, no doubt, to modern times—she has come across our black hero, having entered his room without knocking, holding only a towel between his nakedness and her indignation—"and furthermore to that, you ain't even that handsome!" For she is a part of the family: she would appear to have no family of her own: and is clearly prepared to protect her golden-haired mistress from the clutches of this black ape by any means necessary.

The inclusion of this figure is absolutely obligatory—compulsive—no matter what the film imagines itself to be saying by means of this inclusion. How many times have we seen her! She is Dilsey, she is Mammy, in *Gone with the Wind,* and in *Imitation of Life,* and *The Member of the Wedding*—mother of sorrows, whore and saint, reaching a kind of apotheosis in *Requiem for a Nun.* (And yet, black men have mothers and sisters and daughters who are not like that at all!) In *Guess Who,* her presence is meant to be taken as comic, and the film seems to be using her to suggest that backward people can be found on both sides of the racial fence— a point which can scarcely be made so long as one is sitting on it. In any case, in life, she has a family, she may even have a doctor for a son, and she assuredly does not love the white family so deeply as they are compelled to suppose: she cannot, since she knows how bitterly her black family is endangered by her white one.

Then, there is the scene with the mother and the lady assistant at the art gallery, a scene which Miss Hepburn obviously relishes, and which she plays with a marvelously vindictive skill. The lady assistant is horrified at the news of this impending disastrous marriage, and is full of sympathy for the mother: who reacts with a cold, proud, and even rather terrified contempt. (This is probably the best scene in the film, and it juts out from it because of Hepburn's genuine indignation.) She walks the lady to her car, makes her get into the car, instructs her to pay herself her wages, and a bonus, to start her car motor, to get rid of the artistic monstrosity with which we have seen the doctor amusing himself earlier, and get permanently lost. One down, then, but several more to go, for, now, here come the doctor's father and mother.

The film's high polish does not entirely succeed in blinding us to a kind of incipient reality suggested by these two. Though they come, principally, out of a Hollywood scriptwriter's imagination, they unexpectedly resist being manipulated into total irrelevance—or, in other words, it proved somewhat difficult to find a place for them in this so briefly troubled Eden.

The black mother and the white mother become allies at once, firmly opting for the happiness of their children. The black father and the white father, without becoming allies, nevertheless agree that their children should not marry. I forgot to mention the priest, who is, perhaps, the master stroke of the film. Though, as the film carefully informs us, the Tracy-Hepburn couple are not Catholic, this priest is their best friend, and he is, unequivocally, on the side of the young couple. The two crass, practical fathers find, therefore, that they have taken on those two formidable adversaries, the Church, and mother love—the last being also related to women's intuition. The Church, here, is truculent (rather than militant) and mocks the fears of the white father: and mother love, as projected by Bea Richards in her brief scene with Spencer Tracy, moderately poignant and perceptive. The outcome cannot really very much longer be left in doubt (the film has got to end) but before we can arrive at the film's resolution, there is another matter to be dealt with, and that involves the relationship of the black father to the black son.

It is here that the film's polish cracks—becomes, as it were, unglued. There is no way, simply, for so light and self-serving a fable to deal with a matter so weighty—and so painful. It is not enough for the father to feel that his son has gone mad, and is throwing away his life, or his future, because of a doomed infatuation. The crucial element in such a confrontation is the question—vivid, though nearly unspoken—between the father and the son: what did the father raise the son to respect? For the son can make his lonely decision now only by confronting the nature and the value of that gift. A black man who has raised a son who has achieved his own life, and a son who has also achieved worldly eminence, has great respect for that son. He will offer his judgment, but he will not attempt to impose his will. As for being frightened for that son, the father has been frightened so long that this fear has become no more remarkable to him than the fact that he has to shave; moreover, hiding his fear from his son has been one of the principal conditions of his life, as a father, and a man. And rarely does the father complain about the sacrifices he has made: the subject arrives during adolescence, when the father is attempting to prepare the son for the price *he* will have to pay for his life. All this takes place, anyway, in a kind of short-hand virtually impossible to translate for the bulk of white Americans. But, leaving all that aside, the father has absolutely no motive for this scene. The son is a world-famous doctor, thirty-seven years old, who has already been married, and who has lived all over the world; and who, if he marries the girl, is immediately taking her away with him, out of the United States. The father knows perfectly well that America is not the world: indeed, it would have to be a part of his pride that his effort has helped to release his son from the obscenely crippling pressures of his homeland. It can make absolutely no difference to him who his son marries: if the son is free and happy, the father is, too. And it is worth noting, perhaps, that the film appears completely to forget the wonder doctor's eminence, and the effect that this would have on his parents. As the parents of a world-famous man, they, indisputably, out-rank their hosts, and might very well feel that the far from galvanizing fiancée is not worthy of their son: it is not the black parents who would be ill at ease.

But the American self-evasion, which is all that this country has as history, has created the myth on which this film is based, and this myth cannot endure so treacherous a perception; treacherous to the American self-image, and to what passes, in America, for self-esteem. Only yesterday, if, indeed, it was yesterday, the hotly contested white fiancée cried *death before dishonor!* (or *you*

yellow dogs!) and ran out of this life, into the arms of Jesus, in order not to be defiled by the nigger's touch. Today—if it *is* today—she tells her mother, in a scene manipulated with such cool
efficiency that it almost seems to be true, that, although she certainly wanted to sleep with her black fiancé, *he* was too honorable
to touch *her:* in this day of so many liberations, make of this colli-
sion of inadmissible fantasies whatever you will. In any case, it is
out of all this that the black son must say, finally, to his black
father, and ignobly enough, "You're a colored man. I just want to
be a man." Which means that a man exists only in the brutally
limited lexicon of those who think of themselves as white, and
imagine, therefore, that they control reality and rule the world.
And the black son says this to his black father in spite of the fact
that he, the wonder doctor, has had to become a living freak, a
walking encyclopedia of rare medical knowledge, in order to have
the question of his marriage to a white girl *discussed.* The assump-
tions of *The Last of the Mohicans* and *The Birth of a Nation* are
very present here, and, if even the wonder doctor must undergo
such trials in order to be able to touch his lady love, heaven help
the high-school dropouts: so many of whom found themselves in
Attica, for example, not impossibly for trying to be men. Heaven
did not help those among the blacks who failed to master their
pre-med courses on the day that the Republic, responsive to the
will of heaven, decided to uphold what Rockefeller, in one of his
nobler statements, described as "the impartial application of the
law": he, too, clearly, is a movie fan.

The film does make one despairing attempt to suggest, after
Galileo, that the earth may be turning; in that lamentable scene
in the city when Tracy tastes a new flavor of ice cream and discov-
ers that he likes it. This scene occurs in a drive-in, and is punc-

tuated by Tracy's backing his car into the car of a young black boy. The black boy's resulting tantrum is impressive—and also entirely false, due to no fault of the actor (D'Urville Martin). The moral of the scene is *They're here now, and we have to deal with them:* or, *The natives are restless. What shall we do?*

Ah. What indeed—short, that is, of bombing them back into the stone age. As concerns *Guess Who's Coming to Dinner,* we can conclude that people have the right to marry whom they choose, especially if we know that they are leaving town as soon as dinner is over.

In Sol Stein's *The Childkeeper,* a short and remarkable novel, a forty-eight-year-old bank vice-president, and his wife, and three of their four children, spend a long weekend together in their country house. The children, who are adolescents, invite some of their adolescent friends, and, among these, is a black boy of nineteen, named Greco. The father finds himself paralyzed by his liberal, or, more accurately, humanitarian presumptions (presumptions by which he does not live) and by his apprehension that he really knows nothing about his children, nor (he both hopes and fears) they about him. The presence of the black boy, an exceedingly rude and dangerous visitor, drags to the surface the buried terrors of his life, and, helplessly, he kills the boy. He does not mean to kill him, but Eden has a price: and the death of the black boy brings about his own.

The question of identity is a question involving the most profound panic—a terror as primary as the nightmare of the mortal fall. This question can scarcely be said to exist among the wretched, who know, merely, that they are wretched and who bear it day by day—it is a mistake to suppose that the wretched do not know that they are wretched; nor does this question exist among the splendid, who know, merely, that they are splendid, and who flaunt it, day by day: it is a mistake to suppose that the splendid have any intention of surrendering their splendor. An identity is questioned only when it is menaced, as when the mighty begin to fall, or when the wretched begin to rise, or when the stranger enters the gates, never, thereafter, to be a stranger: the stranger's presence making *you* the stranger, less to the stranger than to yourself. Identity would seem to be the garment with which one covers the nakedness of the self; in which case, it is best that the garment be loose, a little like the robes of the desert, through which robes one's nakedness can always be felt, and, sometimes, discerned. This trust in one's nakedness is all that gives one the power to change one's robes.

Lawrence of Arabia, stemming, both dimly and helplessly, from T. E. Lawrence's *Seven Pillars of Wisdom,* is a kind of muted and updated, excruciatingly astute version of Rudyard Kipling's *Gunga Din.* The word "muted" does not refer to the musical score, which must be the loudest in the history of the cinema, and which is absolutely indispensable to the intention of the film.

The song says *There is trouble all over this world:* and our ancestors, the English, made careful note of this, and proceeded to base their imperial policy on this relentless and utilitarian truth. Living on an island, they built boats, and where trouble was, they sailed them; sometimes, they very carefully brought the needed trouble with them, and very often, simply, their presence was trouble enough. The English learned how to use, and foment, trouble to their purposes, and this policy was known as Divide and Rule. Alongside this, and justifying it, was the concept and necessity of Civilization. I point this out, calmly enough, because nothing in *Lawrence of Arabia* really conveys the fact that the British were deliberately using, and backing, an Arab rebellion in order to complete the dismemberment of the Ottoman Empire. This they managed to do, without keeping any of their promises to the Arabs, to the great sorrow and bewilderment of young Lawrence, who does not understand, until Damascus, to what pragmatic ends his idealism has been put. (The Sykes-Picot Treaty contained a secret clause which divided the conquered territory between England, France, and Russia. Lawrence, in his book, is aware of this. But, "In revenge I vowed to make the Arab revolt the engine of its own success, as well as hand-maid to our Egyptian campaign: and vowed to lead it so madly in the final victory that expediency should counsel to the Powers a fair settlement of the Arabs' moral claims.")

The film begins with a long, overhead shot of a motorcycle in a sunlit square. A khaki-clad man appears and begins fooling around with the motorcycle: walks off, comes back. A closer shot reveals that he is trying to get the motorcycle started. He starts it, gets on it, and we ride with him through the English countryside, on a sunny day. For those who know that Lawrence died in a motorcycle accident, the film is beginning at the end of Lawrence's life: later on, we may ask ourselves why.

The motorcycle goes off the road, crashes. We are then present at Lawrence's funeral, a very impressive one, treated to vehemently conflicting views of him—emanating from the military—and the film begins.

Since the Empire must be kept in the background—and yet, always be present, hence the overwhelming music—the great burden of this film is on the shoulders of Lawrence, played by Peter O'Toole. But the star of the film is the desert: the vast, technicolored backdrop of the desert meant to invest with splendor a stammering tale.

For, this overwhelming desert, though it exists geographically, and was actually filmed by an actual camera crew, sent there for that purpose, is put to a use which is as far from reality as are most of the people we encounter in it. The least real of these people is Lawrence himself. This is not O'Toole's fault: but so grave an adventure can scarcely be ascribed to the vagaries and idealism of a single man. Lawrence's courage and steadfastness are given as admirable, because hard-won—here, the film, unconsciously, rather patronizes Lawrence; his complexities are barely—or, rather, perhaps, endlessly—hinted at, that is to say never illuminated. His rapport with the Arabs is of great use to the British, whose attitude toward him, otherwise, is, at best, ambivalent. The film takes the view that he was a valiant, maverick, naïve and headstrong, brutally broken in battle, and betrayed, less by his country than by his inability to confront—as do his superiors—the hard facts of life: the hard facts of life, in this case, referring, principally, to the limits and exigencies of power. And it would appear to be true that Lawrence's concept of power existed almost entirely on the messianic level—indeed, on a level far more complex and painful than that—but it is almost impossible to pursue this speculation within the confines described by the film.

The film presents us with an inadvertent martyr to the cause of spreading civilization: the speeding of the light to those in darkness. One of the hazards of this endeavor is that of finding oneself in the hands of the infidels. This is what happens to Lawrence in the film (and in a far more fascinating and terrible way in his book). In the film, he is captured by the Turks, refuses the lustful attentions of a Turkish Bey, and is raped by the soldiers. This precipitates his subsequent slaughter of the fleeing Turkish Army. This slaughter destroys his soul, and, though the desert has now claimed him forever, he no longer has any role in the desert, and so must go home to England, dead, to die.

The film begins with the death of Lawrence in order to avoid, whether consciously or not, the deepest and most dangerous implications of this story. We are confronted with a fallen hero, and we trace the steps which lead him to his end. But the zeal which drove Lawrence into the desert does not begin at the point at which we meet him in the film, but farther back than that, in that complex of stratifications called England. Of this, Lawrence himself was most tormentedly aware.

The English can be said to exemplify the power of nostalgia to an uncanny degree. Nothing the world holds, from Australia to Africa, to America, India, to China, to Egypt, appears to have made the faintest imprint on the English soul: wherever the English are is—or will resist, out of perversity, or at its peril, becoming—England. (Not, on the other hand, of course, that it can ever truly *be* England: but it can try.) This is a powerful presumption, but why, then, the ruder recipient cannot but demand, do not the English stay in England? It would appear that this island people need endless corroboration of their worth: and the tragedy of their history has been their compulsion to make the world their mirror, and this to a degree not to be equalled in the history of any other people—and with a success, if that is the word, not to be equalled in the history of any other people. *I liked the things beneath me*—Lawrence, from *Seven Pillars of Wisdom*, is speaking—*and took my pleasures and adventures downward. There seemed a certainty in degradation, a final safety. Man could rise to any height, but there was an animal level beneath which he could not fall. It was a satisfaction on which to rest.*

The necessity, then, of those "lesser breeds without the law"—those wogs, barbarians, niggers—is this: one must not become more free, not become more base than they: must not be used as they are used, nor yet use them as their abandonment allows one to use them: therefore, they must be civilized. But, when they *are* civilized, they may simply "spuriously imitate [the civilizer] back again," leaving the civilizer with "no satisfaction on which to rest."

Thus, it may be said that the weary melancholy underlying *Lawrence of Arabia* stems from the stupefying apprehension that, whereas England may have been doomed to civilize the world, no power under heaven can civilize England. I am using England, at the moment, arbitrarily, simply because England is responsible for Lawrence: but the principle illustrates the dilemma of all the civilizing, or colonizing powers, particularly now, as their power begins to be, at once, more tenuous and more brutal, and their vaunted identities revealed as being dubious indeed. The greater the public power, the greater the private, inadmissible despair; the greater this despair, the greater the danger to all human life. The camera remains on Lawrence's face a long time before he finally cries, *No prisoners!* and leads his men to massacre the Turks. This pause is meant to recall to us the intolerable mortification he has endured, and to make comprehensible the savagery of this English schoolboy.

But the mortification of an English schoolboy, in the desert, at the hands of infidels who refuse to be civilized, cannot be used to justify the bloody course of Empire, or the ruthless stratagems of power: this schoolboy is armed with the weight of a nation, and his mortification is, or should be, nothing to the point. If we grant that the Turks are, also, notoriously bloodthirsty, then we must equally grant that rape is not unknown in English public schools: there *is* no "animal level" beneath which "we" cannot fall. The truth is that Lawrence was deliberately formed and deliberately used, and, at that moment, superbly executed the real intentions of the state which had formed him. So, after all, do most of us, without even knowing it: sometimes, the unexpected results—given the short-sightedness of states, and statesmen— are immediate, immense, and retaliatory. For example, there may, one day, be a film, called *Chamberlain, at Munich,* in which we will learn, for the first time, of the mortifications Chamberlain endured and which compelled him, as Prime Minister of England, to sell, as it turned out, all of Europe to the then German Chancellor, in order to protect his island. Looking for all the world like the schoolboy he never ceased to be, he proclaimed to cheering crowds, upon his return from Munich, *"If at first you don't succeed, try, try again!"*

The crowds were cheering their own impending ordeal: one wonders how many of them survived the rage which their loyal schoolboy, superb epitome of themselves, had just unleashed against them.

In 1952, I was in America, just in time for the McCarthy era. I had never seen anything like it.

If I had ever really been able to hate white people, the era of that dimwitted, good-natured, flamboyant representative of the American people would have been pure heaven: for, not even the most vindictive hatred could have imagined the slimy depths to which the bulk of white Americans allowed themselves to sink: noisily, gracelessly, flatulent and foul with patriotism. Though cowardice was certainly the most vividly recognizable color in the tapestry, it was not mere cowardice one was watching, but something much worse, an absolute panic, absolutely infantile. Truman, the honest haberdasher and machine-made politician, in whose wisdom we had dropped the atomic bomb on Japan, had been elected President the year (1948) that I left America. Subsequently, my countrymen (who were still arguing among themselves as to this relationship—their relationship, that is, to blacks) decided to entrust their lives, their fortunes, and their sacred honor, not once, but twice, to Daddy Warbucks Eisenhower, who had nothing against McCarthy, and who was Papa to Richard Nixon. I began to feel a terrified pity for the white children of these white people: who had been sent, by their parents, to Korea, though their parents did not know why. Neither did their parents know why these miserable, incontestably inferior, rice-eating gooks refused to come to heel, and would not be saved. But *I* knew why. I came from a long line of miserable, incontestably inferior, rice-eating, chicken-stealing, hog-swilling niggers— who had acquired these skills in their flight from bondage—who still refused to come to heel, and who would not be saved. If two and two make four, then it is a very simple matter to recognize that people unable to be responsible for their own children, and who care so little about each other, are unlikely instruments for the salvation of the people whom they permit themselves the luxury of despising as inferior to themselves. Even in the case of Korea, we, the blacks at least, knew why our children were there: they had been sent there to be used, in exactly the same way, and for the same reasons, as the blacks had been so widely dispersed out of Africa—an incalculable investment of raw material in what was not yet known as the common market.

Each time the black discontent erupts within the continental limits of the United States—erupts, that is, to the extent of demanding a "police action"—the Republic claims "outside" interference. It is simply not conceivable that American blacks can be so unhappy (or so bright, or so brave) as seriously to menace the only social order that they know; a social order, moreover, in which they have achieved, or have been given—let's hear both points of view, please!—the highest standard of living of any black people in the world. Apart from pointing out that the black suicide rate began to rise impressively about a quarter of a century ago, we will not otherwise challenge this moving article of faith. Unluckily, Americans remain at the mercy of this misapprehension when attempting to deal with the world. They do not know how their slaves endured, nor how they endure, nor do they know what their slaves know about them—they do not dare to know it: and what they dare not know about Little Black Sambo is precisely what they do not dare to know about the world by which they are surrounded. Thus, the disaster in Korea had to be explained away. American error being unthinkable, and American might not to be questioned, the disaster could be explained away only by a species of *inside* interference: America was not being defeated, it was being betrayed, by disloyal Americans.

A disloyal American was any American who disapproved of the course his government was taking: though it is very important to stress that Charles Lindbergh, for example, who disapproved of the course his government was taking, and who addressed an America First Committee Rally in Madison Square

Garden to prove it, was never considered anything less than a superb and loyal patriot: as is, today, Governor George Wallace, of Alabama, who would have agreed with Colonel Lindbergh that we were fighting on the wrong side. (Lindbergh's wife, the poetess, Anne Morrow Lindbergh, assured us that the inconveniences of the Third Reich—the foul-smelling camps, the ovens, the gas chambers, the slaughter of, among other human beings, the Jews—were "not in themselves the future," merely "scum on the wave of the future.") The American marked as disloyal was always someone whose disagreement with his government might have begun with his apprehension of the role of Franco's Spain, and Mussolini's Italy, and the Italian adventure in Ethiopia: someone who could see what these piratical rehearsals, carried out with the consent, and the power, of the Western world, meant for the future of the world. It was also someone who could see that it had not been Roosevelt, but a global war, necessitating a war economy, which ended the American, and, subsequently, the Western Depression. A disloyal American was anyone who really believed in equal justice under the law, and his testimony may have begun with the Scottsboro Case, or with the Peekskill riot. A disloyal American was anyone who believed it his right, and his duty, to attempt to feed the hungry, and clothe the naked, and visit those in prison, and he may have been fingered, so to speak, by any Southern senator: he was certainly being scrutinized by the late, and much lamented, J. Edgar Hoover, history's most highly paid (and most utterly useless) *voyeur*.

Americans, then, in order to prove their devotion to American ideals, began informing on each other. I had been living in Europe for nearly four years, and knew refugees from precisely this species of moral and actual nightmare, from Germany, Italy,

Spain, and Russia, and Ethiopia: *Give us your poor!* But this species of refugee was not what the hymn of the Statue of Liberty had in mind.

Lives, careers, and loves were smashed on the rock of this cowardice. I was much younger then: the best I can say is that I was appalled, but not—alas—surprised. Still, it was horrible to be confirmed: out of this obscenely fomented hysteria, we are confronted with the nonsense of the pumpkin papers, the self-important paranoia of Whittaker Chambers, such nightshade creatures as Harvey Matusow, Elizabeth Bentley, and Harry Gold, and the breathtaking careers of those remarkable spies, Julius and Ethel Rosenberg: who are about to lose their lives, just the same, in order to astonish, halt, and purify, an erring nation. Yes: and there were others. Some knew it, and some didn't.

I wandered, then, in my confusion and isolation—for almost all the friends I had had were in trouble, and, therefore, in one way or another, *incommunicado*—into a movie, called *My Son, John*. And I will never forget it.

This movie stars Miss Helen Hayes, the late Van Heflin, and the late Robert Walker. Dean Jagger plays the American Legion husband. (Years and years ago, Dean Jagger had appeared in John Wexley's play about the Scottsboro Case, *They Shall Not Die!*: he played the young reporter whose love forces one of the poor white girls to retract her testimony that the black boys had raped her.)

The family is the American family one has seen and seen and seen again on the American screen: the somewhat stolid, but, at bottom, strong, decent, and loving head of the family; the somewhat scatterbrained, but, at bottom, shrewd, loving, and tough wife and mother; and the children of this remarkable unremarkable couple. In *My Son, John,* there are two sons. One of them plays football, which is, literally, all that we ever learn about him. The other son, John, who does not, apparently, play football, has flown the family coop, and has a job in Washington, where he appears to be doing very well. But they don't see very much of him anymore, which causes the mother some distress: she misses her son, John, and this to a somewhat disquieting extent—the movie seems to feel, however, that this morbid worry about the life of her grown son is the normal reaction of any normal American mother.

The mother's distress is considerably augmented by the arrival of the FBI, in the personable person of Van Heflin, who arrives to ask the family discreet questions concerning their maverick relative. Though this FBI agent is the soul of tact and understanding, the mother eventually perceives the gravity of the situation, and agrees to attempt to save her son. The salvation of her son depends on confession, for he is, indeed, a Communist agent: for the sake of her son's salvation, she must, therefore, cooperate with the FBI. For, if her son does not confess, he is lost: he is anathema. The film concentrates on the struggle in the soul of the mother between mother love and her larger duty. At one point in the film, she cheers him on, exactly as though he were in the football field, urging him to make the touchdown and save the team.

Nothing can possibly redeem so grisly a species of sentimental dishonesty, but Robert Walker's gleefully vicious parody of the wayward American son does a great deal to demystify it. The moment he enters the family house, he makes the reasons for his leaving it very clear: his American Legion father, his adoring mother, his football-playing brother, bore him shitless, and he simply does not want to be like them. This is heresy, of course, and Walker plays it for all it is worth, absolutely heartless and hilarious, acting out all of his mother's terrors, including, and especially, the role of flaming faggot, which is his father's terror, too. It is astonishing that he was allowed to get away with so broad and hostile a put-down—one very nearly expects him to turn up, in black-face, singing "Mammy"—but, on the other hand, this is probably exactly the way the film sees wayward sons. Once they have renounced the American virtues, they are, because of this renunciation, practically Communists already and able to incarnate everything we fear.

Virtue triumphs, at last, of course, but not before the erring son has come to a bloody end. He has been sacrificed to life's larger aims, that is, to the American way of life. The mother says to the father, at the close of the film—the father having more swiftly perceived, and faced, his son's defection—*You were more right than any of us, dear, because you thought with your heart.* This meant, in the context of those years—the harvest of which we have not done reaping—that Elizabeth Bentley and Matusow and Greenglass were also thinking with their hearts, and so were the friendly witnesses before the House Un-American Activities Committee, who threw their friends to the wolves, and so was Eisenhower, when he refused to intervene in the Rosenberg case. No crime had been proven against Ethel Rosenberg: she was considered to have masterminded her husband's crimes, though, clearly, there could be no proof of this, either, nor can it be said that there exists any proof of her husband's crimes. Eisenhower, nevertheless, asserted that leniency toward Ethel Rosenberg would mean, simply, that, thereafter, the Russians would recruit their spies from among women. Music up, slow dissolve (exterior, day) to close-up of the Statue of Liberty, fade-out, the end.

My first encounter with the FBI took place in 1945, in Woodstock, New York, where I was living in a cabin in the woods. Neither of the two men resembled Van Heflin in the least.

It was early in the morning, they walked me out of the diner, and stood me against a wall. My color had already made me conspicuous enough in that town—this is putting it mildly indeed—and, from a distance, the townspeople stared. I had the feeling that they were waiting to be selected as members of the firing squad.

I had not the remotest notion as to why they had come looking for me. I knew of nothing which I could possibly have done to have attracted their attention. Much later in my life, I knew very well what I had done to attract their attention, and intended, simply, to keep on keeping on. In any case, once you *have* come to the attention of the FBI, they keep a friendly file on you, and your family, and your friends.

But, on this morning, I was terribly frightened, and I was desperately trying to keep one jump ahead of them—to guess what it was before they revealed it. If I could guess what it was, then I might know how to answer and know what to do.

It developed that they were looking for a boy who had deserted from the Marines. I knew no one answering that description, and I said so. They conveyed, very vividly, what they would do to me if I did not tell them the truth—what they could do to smart niggers like me. (I was a smart nigger because I worked, part-time, as an artists' model, and lived in an artists' colony, and had a typewriter in my shack.) My ass would be in a sling—this was among the gentler warnings. They frightened me, and they humiliated me—it was like being spat on, or pissed on, or gang-raped—but they made me hate them, too, with a hatred like hot ice, and all I knew, simply, was that, if I could figure out what they wanted, nothing could induce me to give it to them.

They showed me a series of photographs. From their questions, I realized that they were talking about something that had taken place in the city, during my last visit there. I had spent a lot of time in the restaurant, where I was still occasional waiter. And I had been to a party, briefly, with some friends of mine. One photograph rang a distant bell in my memory: and they saw this. I had seen the face somewhere, but I could not remember where. And, now, my problem was to remember where I had seen the face, and then double lock the memory out of their reach.

And, eventually, I *did* remember. The boy's name was Teddy. I had met him at a party, with some friends of mine—who were, really, friends of his; had seen him, in fact, only once, and very briefly. If I could scarcely remember his name, he would certainly have the same difficulty with mine, and, if he was a fugitive from justice, he would scarcely take a chance on coming to hide in my cabin.

I knew the name now, and I was determined not to reveal it. It was no part of my duty to help them trap the cat, and, no doubt, he had his reasons for deserting the Marines. But the interrogation was rugged, ruthless, and prolonged, and, eventually, the name slipped out: "Well, there was Carmen, and me, and Joe, and Teddy—"

"Teddy? Is this Teddy?"

I cursed myself, for, of course, they had known the name all along. My utterance of the name had confirmed something, and I had been helpful to them, after all. This frightened me in a new way, in a way that I had never been frightened before. I could see, suddenly, that they could keep me against this wall, under this sun, for the foreseeable future, and, finally, whatever I knew would be dragged out of me. But, in fact, thank God, or somebody, all I knew about the boy was his name. I did not even know his last name. And the afternoon wore on, with threats and curses. They came to my cabin, and searched it—I felt that they had searched it before.

When the interrogation was finally over, one of them took out a nickel and dropped it into my palm. With this nickel, the moment I had any news of Teddy I was to call him. I'd be a mighty sorry nigger if I didn't. I took the nickel, and I assured him that I would certainly call him the moment I had any news of Teddy. I thought, You can bet your ass I'll call you. Don't piss, don't shit, don't fuck, until I call you: do nothing till you hear from me.

They left me, finally, haunted the cabin, and roamed the town for two days. Teddy never appeared. I never spent the nickel, I threw it away.

Teddy was turned in. This, I learned much later, in New York, during my visit in 1952. One of the friends at that long-gone party really knew Teddy, and the FBI had come to see him, too, and had also given him a nickel. I was having dinner with this friend one night, and he told me, in the casual course of conversation, that he believed that Teddy had stolen his typewriter, and this had made him so angry that he had gone downstairs, to the drugstore, and dropped the nickel in the slot, and turned the deserter in.

Well. Perhaps he would have turned him in, anyway—human beings, including you and me, are capable of anything, and *I* might have turned him in. Being human, I certainly have no guarantee that betrayal is not among my possibilities, and, indeed, betrayal takes so many forms that I know myself to have been guilty of betrayal more than once. But I do not think that my friend—with whom I never broke bread again—would have spoken of it so lightly had it not been for the moral climate of the time. The artifacts of the time had helped create this climate, and the artificers of the time had become accomplices to this unspeakable immorality. I was an artificer, too, facing, therefore, a heavy question. I loved my country, but I could not respect it, could not, upon my soul, be reconciled to my country as it was. And I loved my work, had great respect for the craft which I was compelled to study, and wanted it to have some human use. It was beginning to be clear to me that these two loves might, never, in my life, be reconciled: no man can serve two masters.

THREE

Where the Grapes of
Wrath are Stored

> I found a leak in my building,
>   and:
> my soul has got to move.
>   I say:
> my soul has got to move,
> my soul has got to move.
>
> SONG

Aᴛ ᴛʜᴇ ᴛᴏᴘ ᴏꜰ 1968, over the vehement protests of my family and my friends, I flew to Hollywood to write the screenplay for *The Autobiography of Malcolm X.* My family and my friends were entirely right; but I was not (since I survived it) entirely wrong. Still, I think that I would rather be horsewhipped, or incarcerated in the forthright bedlam of Bellevue, than repeat the adventure—not, luckily, that I will ever be allowed to repeat it: it is not an adventure which one permits a friend, or brother, to attempt to survive twice. It was a gamble which I knew I might lose, and which I lost—a very bad day at the races: but I learned something.

Fox was then resolving the Cuban-American tension by means of a movie called *Ché!.* This enterprise gave us Omar Sharif, as Ché Guevara, and Jack Palance, as Fidel Castro: the resulting vaudeville team is not required to sing, or dance, nor is it permitted, using the words very loosely, to act. The United Fruit Company is not mentioned. John Foster Dulles is not mentioned, either, though he was the lawyer for said company, nor is his brother, Allen, who was the head of the CIA. In the person of Ché, we are confronted with a doomed, romantic clown. His attempts to awaken the peasants merely disturb them, and their goats: this observation, which is inexorably and inevitably true on one level, is absolutely false on the level at which the film uses it. In the person of Castro, we are confronted with a cigar-smoking, brandy-drinking maniac: a "spic," as clearly unsuited for political responsibility as the nigger congressmen of *The Birth of a Nation.*

Since both the film for which I had been hired, and *Ché!* were controversial, courageous, revolutionary films, being packaged for the consumer society, it was hoped that our film would beat *Ché!* to the box-office. This was not among my concerns. I had a fairly accurate idea of what Hollywood was about to do with *Ché!.* (This is not black, bitter paranoia, but cold, professional observation: you can make a fairly accurate guess as to the direction a film is likely to take by observing who is cast in it, and who has been assigned to direct it.) The intention of *Ché!* was to make both the man, and his Bolivian adventure, irrelevant and ridiculous; and to do this, furthermore, with such a syrup of sympathy that any incipient Ché would think twice before leaving Mama, and the ever-ready friend at the bank. Ché, in the film, is a kind of Lawrence of Arabia, trapped on the losing side, and unable, even, to understand the natives he has, mistakenly, braved the jungles to arouse. I had no intention of so betraying Malcolm, or *his* natives. Yet, my producer had been advised, in an inter-office

memo which I, quite unscrupulously, intercepted, that the writer
(me) should be advised that the tragedy of Malcolm's life was
that he had been mistreated, early, by some whites, and betrayed
(later) by *many* blacks: emphasis in the original. The writer was
also to avoid suggesting that Malcolm's trip to Mecca could have
had any political implications, or repercussions.

Well. I had never before seen this machinery at such close
quarters, and I confess that I was both fascinated and challenged.
Near the end of my Hollywood sentence, the studio assigned me
a "technical" expert, who was, in fact, to act as my collaborator.
This fact was more or less disguised at first, but I was aware of it,
and far from enthusiastic; still, by the time the studio and I had
arrived at this impasse, there was no ground on which I could
"reasonably" refuse. I liked the man well enough—I had no
grounds, certainly, on which to dislike him. I didn't contest his
"track record" as a screenwriter, and I reassured myself that he
might be helpful: he was signed, anyway, and went to work.

Each week, I would deliver two or three scenes, which he
would take home, breaking them—translating them—into cinematic language, shot by shot, camera angle by camera angle. This
seemed to me a somewhat strangling way to make a film. My
sense of the matter was that the screenwriter delivered as clear a
blueprint as possible, which then became the point of departure
for all the other elements involved in the making of a film. For
example, surely it was the director's province to decide where to
place the camera; and he would be guided in his decision by the
dynamic of the scene. However: as the weeks wore on, and my
scenes were returned to me, "translated," it began to be despair-
ingly clear (to me) that all meaning was being siphoned out of
them. It is very hard to describe this, but it is important that I try.

For example: there is a very short scene in my screenplay in which the central character, a young boy from the country, walks into a very quiet, very special Harlem bar, in the late afternoon. The scene is important because the "country" boy is Malcolm X, the bar is Small's Paradise, and the purpose of the scene is to dramatize Malcolm's first meeting with West Indian Archie—the numbers man who introduced Malcolm to the rackets. The interior evidence of Malcolm's book very strongly suggests a kind of father-son relationship between Archie and Malcolm: my problem was how to suggest this as briefly and effectively as possible.

So, in my scene, as written, Malcolm walks into the bar, dressed in the zoot-suit of the times, and orders a drink. He does not know how outrageously young and vulnerable he looks. Archie is sitting at a table with his friends, and they watch Malcolm, making jokes about him between themselves. But their jokes contain an oblique confession: they see themselves in Malcolm. They have all *been* Malcolm once. He does not know what is about to happen to him, but they do, because it has already happened to them. They have been seeing it happen to others, and enduring what has happened to them, for nearly as long as Malcolm has been on earth. Archie, particularly, is struck by something he sees in the boy. So, when Malcolm, stumbling back from the jukebox, stumbles over Archie's shoes, Archie uses this as a pretext to invite the boy over to the table. And that is all there is to the scene.

My collaborator brought it back to me, translated. It was really the same scene, he explained, but he had added a little action—thus, when Malcolm stumbles over Archie's shoes, Archie becomes furious. Malcolm, in turn, becomes furious, and the scene turns into a shoot-out from *High Noon,* with everybody in the bar taking bets as to who will draw first. In this way, said my collaborator (with which judgment the studio, of course, agreed) everyone in the audience could *see* what Archie saw in Malcolm: he admired the "country boy's" guts.

We are to believe, then, on the basis of the "translated" scene, that a group of seasoned hustlers, in a very hip Harlem bar, allow a child from the country whom nobody knows to precipitate a crisis which may bring the heat down on everybody, and in which the child, by no means incidentally, may lose his life—while they take bets. West Indian Archie is so angry that a child stepped on his shoes that he forgets he has all that numbers money on him, and all those people waiting to be paid—both above and below the line. And, furthermore, this was not at all what Archie saw in Malcolm, nor was it what I wanted the audience to see.

The rewritten scene was much longer than the original scene, and, though it occurs quite early in the script, derailed the script completely. With all of my scenes being "translated" in this way, the script would grow bulkier than *War and Peace,* and the script, therefore, would have to be cut. And I saw how that would work. Having fallen into the trap of accepting "technical" assistance, I would not, at the cutting point, be able to reject it; and the script would then be cut according to the "action" line, and in the interest of "entertainment" values. How I got myself out of this fix doesn't concern us here—I simply walked out, taking my original script with me—but the adventure remained very painfully in my mind, and, indeed, was to shed a certain light for me on the adventure occurring through the American looking-glass.

Lady Sings the Blues is related to the black American experience in about the same way, and to the same extent that Princess Grace Kelly is related to the Irish potato famine: by courtesy. The film pretends to be based on Billie Holiday's autobiography, and, indeed, Billie's book may make a very fine film one day: a day, however, which I no longer expect to live long enough to see. The film that *has* been made is impeccably put together, with an irreproachable professional polish, and has one or two nice moments. It has absolutely nothing to do with Billie, or with jazz, or any other kind of music, or the risks of an artist, or American life, or black life, or narcotics, or the narcotics laws, or clubs, or managers, or policemen, or despair, or love. The script is as empty as a banana peel, and as treacherous.

It is scarcely possible to think of a black American actor who has not been misused: not one has ever been seriously challenged to deliver the best that is in him. The most powerful examples of this cowardice and waste are the careers of Paul Robeson and Ethel Waters. If they had ever been allowed really to hit their stride, they might immeasurably have raised the level of cinema and theater in this country. Their effect would have been, at least, to challenge the stultifying predictable tics of such overrated figures as Miss Helen Hayes, for example, and life, as one performer can sometimes elicit it from another, might more frequently have illuminated our stage and screen. It is pointless, however, to pursue this, and personally painful: Mr. Robeson is declining, in obscurity, and Miss Waters is singing in Billy Graham's choir. They might have been treated with more respect by the country to which they gave so much. But, then, we had to send telegrams to the Mayor of New York City, asking him to call off the cops who surrounded Billie's bedside—looking for heroin in her ice cream—and let the Lady die in peace.

What the black actor has managed to give are moments—indelible moments, created, miraculously, beyond the confines of the script: hints of reality, smuggled like contraband into a maudlin tale, and with enough force, if unleashed, to shatter the tale to fragments. The face of Ginger Rogers, for example, in *Tales of Manhattan,* is something to be placed in a dish, and eaten with a spoon—possibly a long one. If the face of Ethel Waters were placed in the same frame, the face of Little Eva would simply melt: to prevent this, the black performer has been sealed off into a vacuum. Inevitably, therefore, and as a direct result, the white performer is also sealed off and can never deliver the best that is in him, either. His plight is less obvious, but the results can be even more devastating. The black performer knows, at least, what the odds are, and knows that he must endure—even though he has done nothing to deserve—his fate. So does the white performer know this, as concerns himself, *his* possibilities, *his* merit, *his* fate, and he knows this on a somewhat less accessible and more chaotic and intimidating level. James Edwards, dead at the age of fifty-three, in a casting office, was a beautiful actor, and knew, at least, that he was an actor. Veronica Lake was a star, riding very high for a while there: she also died in relative obscurity, but it is doubtful that she knew as much.

The moments given us by black performers exist so far beneath, or beyond, the American apprehensions that it is difficult to describe them. There is the close-up of Sidney Poitier's face, for example, in *The Defiant Ones,* describing how his wife, "she say, be nice. Be nice." Black spectators supply the sub-text—the unspoken—out of their own lives, and the pride and anguish in Sidney's face at that moment strike deep. I do not know what happens in the breasts of the multitudes who think of themselves as white: but, clearly, they hold this anguish far outside themselves. There is the truth to be found in Ethel Waters's face at the end of *Member of the Wedding,* the Juano Hernandez of *Young Man with a Horn* and *Intruder in the Dust,* Canada Lee, in *Body and Soul,* the Rochester of *The Green Pastures* and *Tales of Manhattan,* and Robeson in everything I saw him do. You will note that I am deliberately avoiding the recent spate of so-called black films. I have seen very few of them, and, anyway, it would be virtually impossible to discuss them as films. I suspect their intention to be lethal indeed, and to be the subject of quite another investigation. Their entire purpose (apart from making money; and this money is not for blacks; in spite of the fact that some of these films appear to have been, at least in part, financed by blacks) is to stifle forever any possibility of such moments—or, in other words, to make black experience irrelevant and obsolete. And I may point out that this vogue, had it been remotely serious, had a considerable body of work on which to draw—from *Up From Slavery* to *Let Me Live,* from *The Auto-Biography of an Ex-Colored Man,* and *Cane,* to *Black Boy* to *Invisible Man* to *Blues Child Baby* to *The Bluest Eye* to *Soledad Brother.* An incomplete list, and difficult: but the difficulty is not in the casting.

My buddy, Ava Gardner, once asked me if I thought she could play Billie Holiday. I had to tell her that, though she was certainly "down" enough for it—courageous and honest and beautiful enough for it—she would almost certainly not be allowed to get away with it, since Billie Holiday had been widely rumored to be black, and she, Ava Gardner, was widely rumored to be white. I was not really making a joke, or, if I was, the joke was bitter: for I certainly know some black girls who are much, much whiter than Ava. Nor do I blame the black girls for this, for this utterly inevitable species of schizophrenia is but one of the many manifestations of the spiritual and historical trap, called racial, in which all Americans find themselves and against which some of us, some of the time, manage to arrive at a viable and honorable identity. I was really thinking of black actors and actresses, who would have been much embittered if the role of Billie Holiday had been played by a white girl: but, then, I had occasion to think of them later, too, when the tidal wave of "black" films arrived, using such a staggering preponderance of football players and models.

I had never been a Diana Ross fan, and received the news that she was to play Billie with a weary shrug of the shoulders. I could not possibly have been more wrong, and I pray the lady to accept from me my humble apologies—for my swift, and, alas, understandably cynical reaction. For, indeed, the most exasperating aspect of *Lady Sings the Blues,* for me, is that the three principals—Miss Ross, Billy Dee Williams, and Richard Pryor—are, clearly, ready, willing, and able to stretch out and go a distance not permitted by the film. And, even within this straitjacket, they manage marvelous moments, and a truth which is not in the script is sometimes glimpsed through them. Diana Ross, clearly, respected Billie too much to try to imitate her. She picks up on Billie's beat, and, for the rest, uses herself, with a moving humility and candor, to create a portrait of a woman overwhelmed by the circumstances of her life. This is not exactly Billie Holiday, but it *is* the role as written, and she does much more with it than the script deserves. So does Billy Dee, in the absolutely impossible role of Louis McKay, and so does Richard Pryor, in a role which appears to have been dreamed up by a nostalgic, aging jazz *aficionado.*

The film begins at the end, more or less: titles over, we watch a series of sepia stills of Billie being fingerprinted, and thrown, alone, into a padded cell. We pick up, then, on a gawky colored girl, alone in the streets of Harlem. She has been sent by her mother to a rooming house, which turns out to be a whorehouse. She does not stay there long—packs her bags, and gets dressed, in fact, as a particularly horny and vocal client is getting undressed. She has seen Louis in this establishment, or elsewhere: in any case, she has seen him. She later meets him again, in a dive where she is one of the singers, and where the singer is expected to pick up money off the tables with her, ah, sexual equipment. Billie cannot do this, which has its effect on the two men in her life, Louis, and Piano Man (Richard Pryor). It is at this point that Piano Man dubs her "Lady," and it is at this point that she has her first date with Louis. A few frames later, she is the black singer with a white band, touring the South. (Billie went on the road with Artie Shaw, but the film version of this adventure is not in Billie's book.) On the road, she encounters the Ku Klux Klan, and sees a lynching. One of the members of the band has been offering her drugs, but she has always refused. After the lynching—an image, and a moment, to which we shall return—she succumbs to the friendly pusher, and returns to New York, hooked. Louis tries to get her off drugs, but does not succeed. Desperate for a fix, she pulls a razor on him, to force him to give her her works; after which he asks her to leave his house. Her mother dies, she gets busted—I think, in that order—Louis returns, and helps bring her back to the living. He also realizes that she needs her career, and helps her to begin again. Since she cannot work in New York, they end up on the Coast, with Piano Man. Eventually, Louis has to leave, on business, and to arrange her date in Carnegie Hall. Left alone with Piano Man, she decides that she wants to "cop," and sends him out to buy the junk.

They are broke, and so she gives him a ring, which he is to pawn, to pay for it. Piano Man cops, all right, but doesn't pawn the ring, and doesn't pay for the stuff, and is, therefore, beaten to death before her eyes. The patient and loving Louis comes to the Coast, and brings her back to New York, where she scores a triumph on the Carnegie Hall stage. As Billie is singing, *God Bless the Child*, and as thousands cheer, we learn, from blow-ups of newspaper items behind her, of her subsequent misadventures, and her death at the age of forty-four. And the film fades out, with a triumphant Billie, who is, already, however, unluckily, dead, singing on-stage before a delirious audience—or, rather, two: one in the cinema Carnegie Hall, and one in the cinema where we are seated.

It is not every day that a film crams so much cake down one's throat, and yet leaves one with so much more to swallow.

Now, it is not easy enough to say that the film really has nothing to do with Billie Holiday, since the film's authority—and, therefore, its presumed authenticity—derives from the use of her name. It is not enough to say that the film does not recreate her journey: the question is why the film presents itself as her journey. Most of the people who knew, or saw, or heard Billie Holiday will be dying shortly before, or shortly after, this century dies. (Billie would now be sixty years old.) This film cannot be all that is left of her torment and courage and beauty and grace. And the moments of truth smuggled into the film by the actors form a kind of Rosetta stone which the future will not be able to read, as, indeed, the present cannot.

In the film, we meet Billie on the streets of New York. But we do not know that she was raped at ten, sentenced, as a result, to a "Catholic institution" where she beat her hands to "a bloody damn pulp" when she was locked in with the body of a dead girl. We do not know that she was virtually raped at twelve, and that, at thirteen, she was a "hip kitty." We do not know, from the film, that when she refuses to sleep with the horny and vocal Big Blue, he has her thrown in jail: we know nothing, in fact, of the kind of terror with which this girl lived almost from the time that she was born. The incident with Big Blue is reduced to low comedy, much as is the scene with Billie's mother when she tries on the extravagant hat. Billie's testimony concerning the meaning of this hat is not in the film: "all the big-time whores wore big red velvet hats then—she looked so pretty in it"—nor is the fact that it is the mother who had bought the hat, because "we were going to live like ladies." In the film, Billie auditions as a dancer, and is terrible, and she says so in the book. It is also during this audition that the piano player saves her by snarling, "Girl, can you sing?" and so she sings for the first time in public, and this turns out to be the beginning of her career.

But the scene, as recounted by Billie, and the scene as translated in the film have nothing whatever in common. In the film, for no immediately discernible reason, except, perhaps, ambition, Billie drops into a nearby club, and asks for an audition. She is dressed as Hollywood—though it should certainly know better by now, God knows—persistently imagines cheap whores to dress. She joins the chorus line, disastrously, ending with her black bottom stuck out—after which, etc., she sings, etc.

Billie's testimony is that she and her mother were about to be evicted in the morning and that it was as "cold as all hell that night, and I walked out without any kind of coat." She hits a joint, she is indeed allowed to dance, but solo, "and it was pitiful." Before they throw her out, the piano player does indeed say, " 'Girl, can you sing?'—So I asked him to play 'Trav'lin' All

Alone.' That came closer than anything to the way I felt." And: "when I left the joint that night, I split with the piano player and still took home fifty-seven dollars—I went out and bought a whole chicken and some baked beans."

The scene, in the film, is far from being an improvement on Billie's testimony, and it has two curious results, neither of which is vouched for anywhere in Billie's book. One is the invention of Piano Man, who, according to the film, remains with Billie until his death. According to the book, she scarcely ever sees him again, nor, according to Billie's evidence, does he ever become one of her intimates. It is conceivable, of course, however preposterous, that this figure is meant to suggest a kind of distillation of Lester Young: but I do not have the heart to pursue that line of inquiry. The other result is that the club-owner, a white man, becomes one of Billie's staunchest supporters, and closest friends. The book offers no corroborating evidence of this, either, though Billie speaks with great affection of such people as Tony Pastor and Artie Shaw. But absolutely none of these people are even suggested in the film—these people who were so important to her, along with Pigmeat Markham, and "Pops" Armstrong, and Charlie Barnet—or the jazz atmosphere of that period of Billie's life, and our lives. The film suggests nothing of the terrifying economics of a singer's life, and you will not learn, from the film, that Billie received no royalties for the records she was making then: you will not learn that the music industry is one of the areas of the national life in which the blacks have been most persistently, successfully, and brutally ripped off. If you have never heard of the Apollo Theatre, you will learn nothing of it from this film, nor what Billie's appearances there meant to her, or what a black audience means to a black performer.

Now, obviously, the only way to translate the written word to the cinema involves doing considerable violence to the written word, to the extent, indeed, of forgetting the written word. A film is meant to be seen, and, ideally, the less a film talks, the better. The cinematic translation, nevertheless, however great and necessary the violence it is compelled to use on the original form, is obliged to remain faithful to the intention, and the vision, of the original form. The necessary violence of the translation involves making very subtle and difficult choices. The root motive of the choices made can be gauged by the effect of these choices: and the effect of these deliberate choices, deliberately made, must be considered as resulting in a willed and deliberate act—that is, the film which we are seeing is the film we are intended to see.

Why? What do the filmmakers wish us to learn?

Billie is very honest in her book, she hides nothing. We know the effect of her father's death on her, for example, and how her father died, and how, ultimately, this connected with her singing of "Strange Fruit." We see her relationship with her mother: "I didn't want to hurt her, and I didn't—until three years before she died, when I went on junk." We know, from her testimony, that she was in love with the husband who turned her into a junkie, and we certainly know, from her testimony, that she loved the Louis who did his best to save her. I repeat: her testimony, for that is what we are compelled to deal with, and respect, and whatever others may imagine themselves to know of these matters cannot compare with the testimony of the person who was there.

She testifies, too: "I had the white gowns, and the white shoes. And every night they'd bring me the white gardenias and the white junk. When I was on, I was on and nobody gave me any trouble. No cops, no treasury agents, nobody."

"I got into trouble," says Billie, "when I tried to get off."

Let us see what the film makes of all this: what we are meant to learn.

Billie's father is not in the film, and is mentioned, I think, only once: near the end of the film, when she and Piano Man are high—just before Piano Man is murdered—and they both crack up when Billie says that her father never beat her because he was never home.

In the book, her father is a jazz musician, mainly on the road, who, eventually, leaves home, divorces, and re-marries. But, when he was in town, Billie was able to blackmail him into giving her the rent money for her mother and herself. And she cared about him: "it wasn't the pneumonia that killed him, it was Dallas, Texas. That's where he was, and where he walked around, going from hospital to hospital, trying to get help. But none of them would even so much as take his temperature, or let him in [but] because he had been in the Army, had ruined his lungs and had records to prove it, they finally let him in the Jim Crow ward. By that time, it was too late." And, later: "a song was born which became my personal protest—'Strange Fruit'—when [Lewis Allen] showed me that poem, I dug it right off. It seemed to spell out all the things that had killed Pop."

This is quite forthright, and even contains, if one dares say so, a certain dramatic force. In the film, on the southern road, Billie leaves the bus to go relieve herself in the bushes. Wandering along the countryside, Billie suddenly sees, on the road just before her, grieving black people, and a black body hanging from a tree. The best that one can say for this moment is that it is mistaken, and the worst that it is callously false and self-serving—which may be a rude way of saying the same thing: luckily, it is brief. The scene operates to resolve, at one stroke, several problems, and without in the least involving or intimidating the spectator. The lynch scene is as remote as an Indian massacre, occurring in the same landscape, and eliciting the same response: a mixture of pious horror, and gratified reassurance. The ubiquitous Ku Klux Klan appears, marching beside the bus in which the band is riding. The band is white, and they attempt to hide Billie, making, meanwhile, friendly gestures to their marching countrymen. But Billie, because of the strange fruit she has just seen hanging, is now beside herself, and deliberately makes herself visible, cursing and weeping against the Klan: she, and the musicians, make a sufficiently narrow, entirely cinematic escape. This scene is pure bullshit Hollywood-American fable, with the bad guys robed and the good guys casual: as a result, anyway, of all this unhealthy excitement, this understandable (and oddly reassuring) bitterness, Billie finally takes her first fix, and is immediately hooked.

This incident is not in the book: for the very good reason, certainly, that black people in this country are schooled in adversity long before white people are. Blacks perceive danger far more swiftly, and, however odd this may sound, then attempt to protect their white comrade from his white brothers: they know their white comrade's brothers far better than the comrade does. One of the necessities of being black, and knowing it, is to accept the hard discipline of learning to avoid useless anger, and needless loss of life: every mother and his mother's mother's mother's brother is needed.

The off-screen Billie faced down white sheriffs, and laughed at them, to their faces, and faced down white managers, cops, and bartenders. She was much stronger than this film can have any interest in indicating, and, as a victim, infinitely more complex.

Otherwise, she would never have been able to tell us, so simply, that she sang "Strange Fruit" for her father, and got hooked because she fell in love.

The film cannot accept—because it cannot use—this simplicity. That victim who is able to articulate the situation of the victim has ceased to be a victim: he, or she, has become a threat.

The victim's testimony must, therefore, be altered. But, since no one outside the victim's situation dares imagine the victim's situation, this testimony can be altered only after it has been delivered; and after it has become the object of some study. The purpose of this scrutiny is to emphasize certain striking details which can then be used to quite another purpose than the victim had in mind. Given the complexity of the human being, and the complexities of society, this is not difficult. (Or, it does not appear to be difficult: the endless revisions made in the victim's testimony suggest that the endeavor may be impossible. Wounded Knee comes to mind, along with "Swing Low, Sweet Chariot," and we have yet to hear from My Lai.) Thus, for example, ghetto citizens have been heard to complain, very loudly, of the damage done to their homes during any ghetto uprising, and a grateful Republic fastens on this as a benevolent way of discouraging future uprisings. But the truth is, and every ghetto citizen knows this, that no one trapped in the ghetto owns anything, since they certainly do not own the land. Anyone who doubts this has only to spend tomorrow walking through the ghetto nearest to his.

Once the victim's testimony is delivered, however, there is, thereafter, forever, a witness somewhere: which is an irreducible inconvenience for the makers and shakers and accomplices of this world. These run together, in packs, and corroborate each other. They cannot bear the judgment in the eyes of the people whom they intend to hold in bondage forever, and who know more about them than their lovers. This remote, public, and, as it were, principled, bondage is the indispensable justification of their own: when the prisoner is free, the jailer faces the void of himself.

If *Lady Sings the Blues* pretended to be concerned with the trials of a white girl, and starred, say, the late Susan Hayward *(I'll Cry Tomorrow)* or Bette Davis *(A Stolen Life)* or Olivia de Havilland *(To Each His Own)* or the late Judy Garland *(A Star Is Born)* or any of the current chicks, Billie's love for her father and for the husband who so turned her on would be the film's entire motivation: *the guy that won you/has run off and undone you/that great beginning/has seen its final inning/:* as desperately falsified, but in quite another way. The situations of Lana Turner (in *The Postman Always Rings Twice)* or Barbara Stanwyck (in *Double Indemnity)* or Joan Crawford (in almost anything, but, especially, *Mildred Pierce)* are dictated, at bottom, by the brutally crass and commercial terms on which the heroine is to survive—are dictated, that is, by society. But, at the same time, the white chick is always, somehow, saved or strengthened or destroyed by love— society is out of it, beneath her: it matters not at all that the man she marries, or deserts, or murders, happens to own Rhodesia, or that *she* does: love is all.

But the private life of a black woman, to say nothing of the private life of a black man, cannot really be considered at all. To consider this forbidden privacy is to violate white privacy—by destroying the white dream of the blacks; to make black privacy a black and private matter makes white privacy real, for the first time: which is, indeed, and with a vengeance, to endanger the stewardship of Rhodesia. The situation of the white heroine must never violate the white self-image. Her situation must always transcend the inexorability of the social setting, so that her innocence may be preserved: Grace Kelly, when she shoots to kill, at the end of *High Noon,* for example, does not become a murderess. But the situation of the black heroine, to say nothing of that of the black hero, must always be left at society's mercy: in order to justify white history and in order to indicate the essential validity of the black condition.

Billie's account of her meeting with Louis McKay is very simple, even childlike, and very moving. Louis is asleep on a bench, a whore is lifting his wallet, and Billie prevents this, pretending that Louis, whom she has never seen in her life before, is her old man. And she gives Louis his wallet. Anyone surviving these mean streets knows something about that moment. It is not a moment which the film can afford, for it conveys, too vividly, how that victim, the black, yet refuses to be a victim, has another source of sustenance: Billie's morality, at that moment, indeed, threatens the very foundations of the Stock Exchange.

The film does not suggest that the obsolete and vindictive narcotics laws had anything to do with her fate: does not pick up the challenge implicit in her statement: *When I was on, I was on, and nobody bothered me. . . . I got into trouble when I tried to get off.* Neither does it suggest that the distinction between Big Business and Organized Crime is like the old ad, which asks, *Which twin has the Toni?* The film leaves us with the impression, and this is a matter of choices coldly and deliberately made, that a gifted, but weak and self-indulgent woman, brought about the murder of her devoted Piano Man because she was not equal, either to her gifts, or to the society which had made her a star, and, as the closing sequence proves, adored her.

There was a rite in our church, called *pleading the blood.*

When the sinner fell on his face before the altar, the soul of the sinner then found itself locked in battle with Satan: or, in the place of Jacob, wrestling with the angel. All of the forces of Hell rushed to claim the soul which had just been astonished by the light of the love of God. The soul in torment turned this way and that, yearning, equally, for the light and for the darkness: yearning, out of agony, for reconciliation—and for rest: for this agony is compounded by an unimaginable, unprecedented, unspeakable fatigue. Only the saints who had passed through this fire— the incredible horror of the fainting of the spirit—had the power to intercede, to "plead the blood," to bring the embattled and mortally endangered soul "through." The pleading of the blood was a plea to whosoever had loved us enough to spill his blood for us, that he might sprinkle the soul with his love once more, to give us power over Satan, and the love and courage to live out our days.

One of the songs we sang comes out of the last of the Egyptian plagues, the death of the firstborn: *when I see the blood, I will pass over you.* (There is a reason that blacks call each other "bloods.") Another of the songs is, at once, more remote, and yet more present: *somebody needs you, Lord, come by here!*

I had been prayed through, and I, then, prayed others through: had testified to having been born again, and, then, helped others to be born again.

The word "belief" has nearly no meaning anymore, in the

recognized languages, and ineptly approaches the reality to which I am referring: for there can be no doubt that it is a reality. The blacks had first been claimed by the Christian church, and then excluded from the company of white Christians—from the fellowship of Christians: which taught us all that we needed to know about white Christians. The blacks did not so much use Christian symbols as recognize them—recognize them for what they were before the Christians came along—and, thus, reinvested these symbols with their original energy. The proof of this, simply, is the continued existence and authority of the blacks: it is through the creation of the black church that an unwritten, dispersed, and violated inheritance has been handed down. The word "revelation" has very little meaning in the recognized languages: yet, it is the only word for the moment I am attempting to approach. This moment changes one forever. One is confronted with the agony and the nakedness and the beauty of a power which has no beginning and no end, which contains you, and which you contain, and which will be using you when your bones are dust. One thus confronts a self both limited and boundless, born to die and born to live. The creature is, also, the creation, and responsible, endlessly, for that perpetual act of creation which is both the self and more than the self. One is set free, then, to live among one's terrors, hour by hour and day by day, alone, and yet never alone. *My soul is a witness!*—so one's ancestors proclaim, and in the deadliest of the midnight hours.

To live in connection with a life beyond this life means, in effect—in truth—that, frightened as one may be, and no matter how limited, or how lonely, and no matter how the deal, at last, goes down, no man can ever frighten you. This is why blacks can be heard to say, *I ain't* got *to do nothing but stay black, and die!:*

which is, after all, a far more affirmative apprehension than *I'm free, white, and twenty-one.* The first proposition is changeless, whereas the second is at the mercy of time, weather, the dictionary, geography, and fashion. The custodian of an inheritance, which is what blacks have had to be, in Western culture, must hand the inheritance down the line. So, you, the custodian, recognize, finally, that your life does not belong to you: nothing belongs to you. This will not sound like freedom to Western ears, since the Western world pivots on the infantile, and, in action, criminal delusions of possession, and of property. But, just as *love is the only money,* as the song puts it, so this mighty responsibility is the only freedom. Your child does not belong to you, and you must prepare your child to pick up the burden of his life long before the moment when you must lay your burden down.

But the people of the West will not understand this until everything which they now think they have has been taken away from them. In passing, one may observe how remarkable it is that a people so quick and so proud to boast of what they have taken from others are unable to imagine that what they have taken from others can also be taken from them.

In our church, the Devil has many faces, all of them one's own. He was not always evil, rarely was he frightening—he was, more often, subtle, charming, cunning, and warm. So, one learned, for example, never to take the easy way out: whatever looked easy was almost certainly a trap. In short, the Devil was that mirror which could never be smashed. One had to look into the mirror every day—*good morning, blues/ Blues, how do you do?/ Well, I'm doing all right/ Good morning/ How are you?*—check it all out, and take it all in, and travel. The pleading of the blood was not, for us, a way of exorcising a Satan whom we knew could never sleep: it was to engage Satan in a battle which we knew could never end.

I first saw *The Exorcist,* in Hollywood, with a black friend of mine, who had his own, somewhat complex reasons for insisting that I see it: just so, one of my brothers had one day walked me into the film, *The Devils,* which he had already seen, saying, cheerfully, as we walked out, *Ain't that some shit? I just wanted you to see how sick these people are!* Both my friend and my brother had a point. I had already read *The Devils;* now, I forced myself to read *The Exorcist*—a difficult matter, since it is not written; then, I saw the film again, alone. I tried to be absolutely open to it, suspending judgment as totally as I could. For, after all, if I had once claimed to be "filled" with the Holy Ghost, and had once really believed, after all, that the Holy Ghost spoke through me, I could not, out of hand, arbitrarily sneer at the notion of demonic possession. The fact that I had been an adolescent boy when I believed all this did not really get me off the hook: I can produce no documents proving that I am not what I was.

My friend and I had a drink together, after we had seen the film, and we discussed it at some length. He was most struck by the figure of the young priest: he found the key to this personage in a rather strange place, and his observation haunted me for weeks. Father Karras confesses, at one point, that he has lost his faith. "So, we must be careful," David said to me, "lest we lose our faith—and become possessed." He was no longer speaking of the film, nor was he speaking of the church.

I carried this somewhat chilling admonition away with me. When I saw the film again, I was most concerned with the audience. I wondered what they were seeing, and what it meant to them.

The film, or its ambience, reminded me of *The Godfather,* both being afflicted with the same pious ambiguity. Ambiguity is not quite the word, for the film's intention is not at all ambiguous; yet, hypocrisy is not quite the word, either, since it suggests a more deliberate and sophisticated level of cunning. *The Exorcist* is desperately compulsive, and compulsive, precisely, in the terror of its unbelief. The vast quantities of tomato paste expended in *The Godfather* are meant to suggest vast reservoirs of courage, devotion, and nobility, qualities with which the film is not in the least concerned—and which, apart from Brando's performance, are never present in it. (And, at that, it is probably more accurate to speak of Brando's *presence,* a pride, an agony, an irreducible dignity.) *The Exorcist* has absolutely nothing going for it, except Satan, who is certainly the star: I can say only that Satan was never like that when he crossed *my* path (for one thing, the evil one never so rudely underestimated me). His concerns were more various, and his methods more subtle. *The Exorcist* is not in the least concerned with damnation, an abysm far beyond the confines of its imagination, but with property, with safety, tax shelters, stocks and bonds, rising and falling markets, the continued invulnerability of a certain class of people, and the continued sanctification of a certain history. If *The Exorcist* itself believed this history, it could scarcely be reduced to so abject a dependence on special effects.

In Georgetown, in Washington, D.C., a young movie actress is shooting a film. She is forthright, and liberated, as can be gathered from her liberated language. The film she is making is involved with a student uprising—in the book, she describes it as *"dumb!"*: in the film, one of her lines suggests that the students work within the system. This line, however, is neatly balanced by another, which suggests that the political perceptions of this film-within-a-film may owe a great deal to Walt Disney.

Before this, we have encountered the aged priest, who will become the exorcist, digging in the ruins of northern Iraq. This opening sequence is probably the film's most effective, ruthlessly exploiting the uneasiness one cannot but feel when touched by the energy of distant gods, unknown. It sets up, with some precision, the spirit of the terror which informs the Christian-pagan argument: it may be something of a pity that Ingmar Bergman could not have guided the film from there. However, Max von Sydow, the exorcist—rather like Marlon Brando, in *The Godfather*—having been exhibited, is now put on ice, and, if we wish to await his return, we have no choice but to see the end of the movie.

The horror of the demonic possession begins with what sound, to the heroine, like rats in the attic. Her daughter's dresses are misplaced. Room temperatures change, alarmingly and inexplicably. Furniture is mysteriously moved about. Her daughter's personality changes, and obscenities she has never used before become a part of her speech. (Though she overhears the mother using some of them: over the trans-Atlantic telephone, to her father, who is estranged from her mother.) The daughter also plays around with a ouija board, and has made a friend in the spirit world, called Captain Howdy. The mother worries over all these manifestations, both worldly and other-worldly, of the mysteries now being confronted by her growing daughter with all of the really dreadful apathy of the American middle class, reassuring herself that nothing she has done, or left undone, has irreparably damaged her child; who will certainly grow up, therefore, to be as healthy as her mother and to make as much money. But, eventually, at a very posh Georgetown party, of which her mother is the hostess, this daughter comes downstairs in her nightgown, and, while urinating on the floor, tells a member of the party that he is going to die. After this, her affliction, or possession, develops apace.

The plot now compels us to consider a Jesuit priest, young, healthy, athletic, intelligent, presumably celibate, with a dying mother, and in trouble with his faith. His mother dies, alone, in a dingy flat in New York, where he has been compelled to leave her, and he is unable to forgive himself for this. There is the film director, a drunken, cursing agnostic, other priests, psychiatrists, doctors, a detective—well: all people we have met before, and there is very little to be said about them. One of the psychiatrists is nearly castrated by Regan, the daughter, who has abnormal strength while in the grip of Satan. Along with the mumbo-jumbo of levitating beds and discontented furniture and Wuthering Heights tempests, there is the moment when the daughter is compelled by Satan to masturbate with a crucifix, after which she demands that her mother lick her, after which she throws her mother across the room, after which the mother screams, after which she faints. It develops that the film director, dead in a mysterious accident, has actually been pushed: by Regan, through her bedroom window, to his death: again, while in the grip of Satan. All else having failed, the aged priest is called from his retreat to perform the exorcism: the young priest is his assistant. The strain of exorcising Satan proves too much for the aged priest, who has a heart attack, and dies. The young priest, still made with guilt concerning the death of his mother, taunts

Satan, daring him to stop picking on helpless little girls, and enter *him*. Satan does this with an eagerness which suggests that he, too, is weary of little girls and hurls the priest through the bedroom window, to his death, and, also, presumably, to eternal damnation; as to this last point, however, I really cannot be clear.

The young priest is tormented by guilt, and especially in reference to his mother, throughout the film: and Satan ruthlessly plays on this, sometimes speaking (through Regan) in the mother's voice, and sometimes incarnating her. And Satan also plays on the guilt of Regan's mother—her guilt concerning her failed marriage, her star status, her ambition, her relation to her daughter, her essentially empty and hypocritical and totally unanchored life: in a word, her emancipation. This uneasy, and even terrified guilt is the subtext of *The Exorcist*, which cannot, however, exorcise it since it never confronts it.

But this confrontation would have been to confront the devil. The film terrified me on two levels. The first, as I have tried to indicate, involved my deliberate attempt to leave myself open to it, and to the extent, indeed, of re-living my adolescent holy-roller terrors. It was very important for me not to pretend to have surmounted the pain and terror of that time of my life, very important not to pretend that it left no mark on me. It marked me forever. In some measure I encountered the abyss of my own soul, the labyrinth of my destiny: these could never be escaped, to challenge these imponderables being, precisely, the heavy, tattered glory of the gift of God.

To encounter oneself is to encounter the other: and this is love. If I know that my soul trembles, I know that yours does, too: and, if I can respect this, both of us can live. Neither of us, truly, can live without the other: a statement which would not sound so banal if one were not endlessly compelled to repeat it, and, further, believe it, and act on that belief. My friend was quite right when he said, *So, we must be careful—lest we lose our faith—and become possessed.*

For, I have seen the devil, by day and by night, and have seen him in you and in me: in the eyes of the cop and the sheriff and the deputy, the landlord, the housewife, the football player: in the eyes of some junkies, the eyes of some preachers, the eyes of some governors, presidents, wardens, in the eyes of some orphans, and in the eyes of my father, and in my mirror. It is that moment when no other human being is real for you, nor are you real for yourself. This devil has no need of any dogma—though he can use them all—nor does he need any historical justification, history being so largely his invention. He does not levitate beds, or fool around with little girls: *we* do.

The mindless and hysterical banality of the evil presented in *The Exorcist* is the most terrifying thing about the film. The Americans should certainly know more about evil than that; if they pretend otherwise, they are lying, and any black man, and not only blacks—many, many others, including white children—can call them on this lie; he who has been treated *as* the devil recognizes the devil when they meet. At the end of *The Exorcist,* the demon-racked little girl murderess kisses the Holy Father, and she remembers nothing: she is departing with her mother, who will, presumably, soon make another film. The grapes of wrath are stored in the cotton fields and migrant shacks and ghettoes of this nation, and in the schools and prisons, and in the eyes and hearts and perceptions of the wretched everywhere, and in the ruined earth of Vietnam, and in the orphans and the widows, and in the old men, seeing visions, and in the young men, dreaming dreams: these have already kissed the bloody cross and will not bow down before it again: and have forgotten nothing.

ST. PAUL DE VENCE

JULY 29, 1975

ALSO BY JAMES BALDWIN

THE AMEN CORNER

For years Sister Margaret Alexander has moved her congregation with a mixture of personal charisma and ferocious piety. But when her estranged husband, Luke, comes home to die, she is in danger of losing both her standing in the church and the son she has tried to keep on the godly path. *The Amen Corner* is an uplifting, sorrowful, and exultant masterpiece of the modern American theater.

Drama

ANOTHER COUNTRY

Set in Greenwich Village, Harlem, and France, among other locales, *Another Country* is a novel of passions—sexual, racial, political, artistic—that is stunning for its emotional intensity and haunting sensuality, depicting men and women, blacks and whites, stripped of their masks of gender and race by love and hatred at their most elemental and sublime.

Fiction/Literature

BLUES FOR MISTER CHARLIE

In a small Southern town, a white man murders a black man, then throws his body in the weeds. With this act of violence Baldwin launches an unsparing and at times agonizing probe of the wounds of race. For where once a white storekeeper could have shot a "boy" like Richard Henry with impunity, times have changed. In *Blues for Mister Charlie*, Baldwin turns a murder and its aftermath into an inquest in which even the most well-intentioned whites are implicated—and in which even a killer receives his share of compassion.

Fiction/Literature

THE FIRE NEXT TIME

A national bestseller when it first appeared in 1963, *The Fire Next Time* galvanized the nation and gave passionate voice to the emerging civil rights movement. At once a powerful evocation of James Baldwin's early life in Harlem and a disturbing examination of the consequences of racial injustice, the book is an intensely personal and provocative document.

Social Science/African American Studies

The men and women in these eight short fictions grasp this truth on an elemental level, and their stories, as told by James Baldwin, detail the ingenious and often desperate ways in which they try to keep their heads above water. It may be the heroin that a down-and-out jazz pianist uses to face the terror of pouring his life into an inanimate instrument. It may be the brittle piety of a father who can never forgive his son for his illegitimacy. Or it may be the screen of bigotry that a redneck deputy has raised to blunt the awful childhood memory of the day his parents took him to watch a black man being murdered by a gleeful mob. By turns haunting, heartbreaking, and horrifying—and informed throughout by Baldwin's uncanny knowledge of the wounds racism has left in both its victims and its perpetrators—*Going to Meet the Man* is a major work by one of our most important writers.

Fiction/Literature

IF BEALE STREET COULD TALK

In this honest and stunning novel, James Baldwin has given America a moving story of love in the face of injustice. Told through the eyes of Tish, a nineteen-year-old girl in love with Fonny, a young sculptor who is the father of her child, Baldwin's story mixes the sweet and the sad. Tish and Fonny have pledged to get married, but Fonny is falsely accused of a terrible crime and imprisoned. Their families set out to clear his name, and as they face an uncertain future, the young lovers experience a kaleidoscope of emotions—affection, despair, and hope. In a love story that evokes the blues, where passion and sadness are inevitably intertwined, Baldwin has created two characters so alive and profoundly realized that they are unforgettably ingrained in the American psyche.

Fiction/Literature

NO NAME IN THE STREET

A searing memoir and an extraordinary history of the turbulent sixties and early seventies, *No Name in the Street* is James Baldwin's powerful commentary on the political and social agonies of America's contemporary history. The prophecies of *The Fire Next Time* have tragically been realized—through assassinations, urban riots, and increased racial polarization—and the hope for justice seems more elusive than ever. Through it all, Baldwin's uncompromising vision and his fierce disavowal of despair are ever present in this eloquent and personal testament to his times.

Nonfiction

NOBODY KNOWS MY NAME

Nobody Knows My Name is a collection of illuminating, deeply felt essays on topics ranging from race relations in the United States—including a passionate attack on William Faulkner for his ambivalent views about the segregated South—to the role of the writer in society, with personal accounts of such writers as Richard Wright and Norman Mailer.

Literature/African-American Studies

ONE DAY WHEN I WAS LOST

Honor student, revolutionary, street hustler, minister of the Nation of Islam, husband, and father—Malcolm X was one of the most feared, loved, and charismatic American leaders of the 1960s. In this vividly composed gem—his only screenplay—James Baldwin's cinematic vision brings to light a man who changed himself in order to change his country, and richly renders the tumu   ltuous times in which Malcolm lived and died.

Drama

TELL ME HOW LONG THE TRAIN'S BEEN GONE

In this magnificently passionate, angry, and tender novel, James Baldwin created one of his most striking characters, a man struggling to become himself even as he juggles multiple identities—as black man, bisexual, and artist—on the mercilessly floodlit stage of American public life. At the height of his theatrical career, the actor Leo Proudhammer is nearly felled by a heart attack. As he hovers between life and death, Baldwin shows the choices that have made him enviably famous and terrifyingly vulnerable. For between Leo's childhood on the streets of Harlem and his arrival into the intoxicating world of the theater lies a wilderness of desire and loss, shame and rage. An adored older brother vanishes into prison. There are love affairs with a white woman and a younger black man, each of whom will make irresistible claims on Leo's loyalty. And everywhere there is the anguish of being black in a society that at times seems poised on the brink of total racial war.

Fiction/Literature